SUTTON POCKET HISTORIES

THE RUSSIAN REVOLUTION

HAROLD SHUKMAN

SUTTON PUBLISHING

First published in the United Kingdom in 1998 by
Sutton Publishing Limited · Phoenix Mill
Thrupp · Stroud · Gloucestershire · GL5 2BU

British Library Cataloguing in Publication Data
A catalogue record for this book is available from the British
Library.

ISBN 0-7509-1951-5

*Cover picture: Detail from a Communist International poster, 1920
(The David King Collection).*

 ALAN SUTTON™ and SUTTON™ are the
trade marks of Sutton Publishing Limited

Typeset in 11/16 pt Baskerville.
Typesetting and origination by
Sutton Publishing Limited.
Printed in Great Britain by
The Guernsey Press Company Limited,
Guernsey, Channel Islands.

*In loving memory of my father David
and his brother Israel,
who were there*

Contents

	Preface	vii
	List of Dates	ix
1.	Russian Society before the Revolution	1
2.	War	23
3.	The February/March Revolution	35
4.	October	51
5.	Civil War	61
6.	The New Regime	77
7.	The Cultural Revolution	99
	Postscript	105
	Notes	107
	Further Reading	109
	Index	111

Preface

Although the Soviet Union no longer exists – and even if it comes to be seen as no more than 'the socialist era' in the long history of Russia – few events in the turbulent twentieth century have had such a lasting and deep impact as the Russian Revolution of 1917 that brought it into being. The revolution launched new ways of thinking about and practising economic, social and political organization. The Bolsheviks saw society in sharply divided terms: exploited and exploiters, labour and capital, proletarian and bourgeois, good and evil; and they set out to accomplish on a worldwide scale what they believed they were going to achieve in Russia – a socialist revolution that would sweep away all injustices arising from these differences.

The Russian Revolution began with the removal of a 300-year old dynasty and went on in a series of increasingly chaotic steps to the seizure of power eight months later by a relatively small body of armed revolutionaries. The first of these two stages began with a revolt on 8 to 12 March, when confidence in the tsar's ability to defend the country in the First

World War finally drained away, and support for the continuation of the monarchy as such evaporated. The second stage occurred in October when Lenin, the only political leader rash, or audacious, enough to promise an immediate end to the war, seized power from Alexander Kerensky, the leader of a Provisional Government that had all but fizzled out.

An event as momentous as the Russian Revolution, however, cannot be explained as the actions of one man, whether it was those of Nicholas II or of Lenin. It is certainly true that the personality of Nicholas played a vital part in the collapse of his regime, as to some extent did that of Kerensky in the demise of the Provisional Government which he led, and it is equally true that the Bolshevik seizure of power would not have occurred as and when it did if Lenin had not been present in Petrograd. But Russia had been experiencing social turmoil and political upheaval for many years and the events of 1917 should be seen as the culmination of a long process, rather than a sudden and unexpected eruption.

List of Dates

Until February 1918 dates in Russia conformed to the Julian or Old Style calendar which was lagging behind the Gregorian Western, or New Style, by twelve days in the nineteenth century and by thirteen in the twentieth century. Thus, the February Revolution of 1917 took place in March according to the Western calendar and the Bolsheviks seized power on 25 October 1917, when in the West the date was 7 November. We have cited both dates to avoid ambiguity.

1870 **April 10/22**. Vladimir Ulyanov (Lenin) born in Simbirsk.

1881 **March 1/12**. Alexander II assassinated in St Petersburg.

1883 Formation in Geneva of first Russian Marxist group, the Group for the Emancipation of Labour.

1896 **May 14/26**. The coronation of Nicholas II.

1898 **March 1/12**. Russian Social Democratic Workers' Party founded in Minsk.

1902 Socialist Revolutionary Party (SRs) founded in Geneva.

1903 Summer Social Democratic Party splits into Bolsheviks and Mensheviks at its Second Congress in Brussels and London.

1904 **January**. Japan launches a surprise attack on Russian warships at Port Arthur.

1905 **9/22 January**. Bloody Sunday in St Petersburg opens the
year of revolution.
August. Nicholas II promises constitution. Formation of
St Petersburg Workers' Soviet.
October. Imperial Manifesto announces elections to State
Duma.
December. Suppression of armed rising in Moscow.

1906 **January**. Convocation of First State Duma; Stolypin
becomes Prime Minister.

1907 **March**. Convocation of Second State Duma (of three
months' duration).
June 6/13. Convocation of Third State Duma.

1911 **September**. Stolypin assassinated in presence of Nicholas
II in Kiev.

1912 **April**. Massacre of miners at Lena gold fields in Siberia.
Rasputin's scandalous behaviour debated in Duma.
September. Convocation of Fourth State Duma.

1914 **August**. Germany declares war on Russia. St Petersburg
renamed Petrograd. German embassy burnt down.

1915 **August**. Nicholas II becomes Commander-in-Chief. Duma
members form Progressive Bloc.

1916 **30 December**/12 January 1917. Rasputin murdered.

1917 **January–February**. Strikes and demonstrations in
Petrograd.
12 March. Petrograd Soviet of Workers' Deputies formed.
13 March. Soviet issues Order No. I.
14 March. Nicholas abdicates. Provisional Government
formed under Prince Lvov.
3/16 April. Lenin returns to Russia via Scandinavia and
calls for 'All Power to the Soviets'.

May. Collapse of first Provisional Government. Formation of second Provisional Government including six socialist ministers, with Kerensky as Minister for War.

3/16 June. First All-Russian Congress of Workers' and Soldiers' Deputies opens in Petrograd.

2/17 July. Trotsky joins the Bolsheviks. Kerensky orders arrest of Lenin and Bolshevik leaders on charges of spying for the Germans; Lenin goes into hiding.

8/21 July. Kerensky becomes Prime Minister.

16/29 July. Kornilov appointed Commander-in-Chief.

September. Kornilov's attempted coup defeated. Trotsky becomes chairman of Petrograd Soviet Bolshevik majorities in Petrograd and Moscow Soviets; Lenin revives slogan of 'All Power to the Soviets'.

10/23 October. Lenin chairs Bolshevik Central Committee which approves his call for an armed uprising.

24–5 October/6–7 November. Red Guards seize key building and installations in capital.

25 October/7 November. Provisional Government ministers arrested. Bolshevik coup announced at Second Congress of Soviets.

27 October/9 November. Congress of Soviets passes Lenin's decrees on land and peace and appoints first Soviet government, the Council of People's Commissars, with Lenin as chairman.

27 October/9 November. Press decree outlaws opposition press.

2/15 November. Bolsheviks take power in Moscow.

12/25 November. Month-long elections to Constituent Assembly begin.

20 November/3 December. Armistice talks begin at Brest-Litovsk.

22 November/5 December. Courts and legal profession abolished. Revolutionary tribunals created.

26 November/6 December. Armistice agreed.

7/20 December. Cheka established.

9/22 December. Left SRs join government.

December/January. Volunteer Army formed by Generals Alexeyev and Kornilov.

1918 **5/18 January**. Opening of the Constituent Assembly.

6/19 January. Bolsheviks disperse Constituent Assembly by force

8/21 January. Soviet Russian Republic proclaimed.

9/22 February. Central Powers sign separate with independent Ukraine; Germany issues ultimatum at Brest-Litrovsk.

18 February/3 March. Central Powers resume offensive against Russia.

1/14 March. Russian delegation accepts Germany's peace terms; Left SRs leave government.

14 March. Bolshevik government transfers to Moscow.

22 March. Intervention forces land at Murmansk.

April. Japanese forces land at Vladivostok.

May. All property nationalized.

May/June. Bolsheviks lose majorities in all urban soviets and reimpose them by force.

June. Grand Duke Michael murdered.

4 July. First Soviet Constitution approved.

6 July. Left SR uprising in Moscow.

16 July. Murder of Nicholas II and family in Yekaterinburg.

30 August. Assassination attempt on Lenin.

September. Official launch of Red Terror; massacre of prisoners and hostages.

October. Lenin orders destruction of all property title deeds.

13 November. Lenin renounces Treaty of Brest-Litovsk.

1919 **March**. Bolshevik Party renamed Russian Communist Party.

April. Concentration camps introduced.

April. Polish forces invade Ukraine.

June. Red Army drives Poles from Ukraine.

August. Red Army defeated at Warsaw.

18 October. Armistice with Poland.

1921 **February**. Mass strike in Petrograd.

28 February. Mutiny at Kronstadt.

March. Tenth Party Congress introduces NEP and bans Party factions.

17 March. Red Army crushes Kronstadt revolt.

August. Government asks for food aid; American Relief Administration arrives in Soviet Russia.

1922 **25 May**. Lenin suffers a stroke.

August. Large numbers of intellectuals deported abroad.

15 December. Lenin suffers second stroke.

December/January. Lenin dictates 'Testament'.

1923 **10 March**. Lenin paralyzed.

1924 **21 January**. Lenin dies.

ONE

Russian Society before the Revolution

By the beginning of this century a great part of
Russian society sensed that important changes were
imminent. Whether this expectancy was no more
than the result of a new millennium, or of the
awareness that Russia was being left behind as the
Western world erupted with new ideas in all
branches of human endeavour, or was merely
wishful thinking, the fact is the feeling was
widespread and mounting.

Young educated Russians in particular gave vent
to this feeling. Many were committed, intellectually
and in many cases in practice, to the cause of
socialist revolution. Most believed that their mission
was to open the eyes of the workers and peasants to
the causes of their hardship, to help them organize
themselves to alleviate that hardship and take their

place as a political class with full equality, and ultimately to become the ruling class and build socialism.

Others took a more extreme position, advocating terrorism against high officials as a means of destabilizing the state and stirring up rebellion. These tactics failed in both aims and tended, on the contrary, to promote a defensive attitude among large sections of the educated and uneducated population alike.

A third section of disaffected youth adopted the course of forming an organization consisting of a network of illegal secret committees inside Russia, coordinated from abroad by a political centre and controlled by itinerant agents. The aims of this organization were to instil Marxist social democratic and revolutionary ideas into the working class, and create a party on a national scale whose goal was to take power in the name of the working class, or proletariat.

The Russian Social Democratic Workers' Party was founded in Minsk in 1897 and split in 1903 into two wings called Mensheviks and Bolsheviks, or Minorityites and Majorityites. The split was not popular among social democrats inside Russia, who viewed it as the sectarian fetishism of idle intellectuals who were enjoying the luxury of residence abroad, while they, the workers, had to endure the hardships of Russian industrial life and the harassment of the security police, and for several years thereafter many committees refused to split and insisted on calling themselves 'united'.

Essentially the Mensheviks believed that the tsarist regime should be succeeded by a liberal democratic order that would put all classes on a level political and legal playing field. The Russian workers, they argued, were not ready to play a political role and should concentrate on organizing themselves, while they, the Mensheviks, would help them wrest a higher standard of living from the employers. When the workers were ready to make a bid for power the Mensheviks would be there to give political leadership. Meanwhile the Social Democratic Party should gather support from all sectors of society and take advantage of all legally permitted activities to broadcast its values widely. Although their membership – like that of their Bolshevik rivals – declined dramatically following the defeat of the 1905 revolution, the Mensheviks were successful in becoming embedded in labour organizations and embedding their ideas deep into the workers' minds.

The Bolsheviks were led by Vladimir Ulyanov,

better known as Lenin. Born in 1870 into the family of a middle-ranking schools' inspector in the provincial town of Simbirsk, Lenin soon gained the reputation of the most obsessed of revolutionaries – a man who lived and dreamed of nothing but revolution. Inspired by his powerful ideological drive the Bolsheviks also did not believe that the workers were capable of engaging in politics. Instead they saw them as a potentially violent force to be thrown against the existing order in time of crisis. Thus, throughout the period up to the 1917 revolution itself, the Bolsheviks maintained a militantly revolutionary stance, trying to ensure that neither the Mensheviks nor the liberals captured the political leadership of the left. Lenin's idea of the party was that it should be a disciplined, tightly enclosed organization of what he called professional revolutionaries. He obsessively fought a continuous battle against those of his own comrades who wanted to broaden the revolutionary front by collaborating with the Mensheviks and in the years following the defeat of the 1905 revolution he became isolated even among the Bolsheviks.

In the early years of the century even respectable citizens of moderate views shared the belief that radical changes were going to take place in the social order. What had given rise to this radical mood and to what extent was it responsible for the changes that eventually occurred? In order to address these questions, it is useful to examine the composition of Russian society and to identify the problems being faced across the spectrum in the years leading up to the change of regime.

PEASANTS

In 1861 the serfs were emancipated by Alexander II in a spirit of enlightened reform. In moral terms the act aimed at ending what had come to be seen as an abuse of human rights. In economic terms it was intended to create a large class of independent and self-reliant farmers and to release a pool of new labour for industrial development. But as the tsar also wanted to secure both tax collection and a supply of recruits for his large standing army, he decreed that peasants must be registered as members of a commune – in practice, their own native village – which would bear responsibility for both these public duties. He also left it to local landowners to determine the value, as well as the quantity, of the land they were required to hand over to the peasants by the terms of the emancipation. The state paid the former serf-owner for the land so surrendered and the peasant was obligated to redeem the debt to the state in forty-nine years.

In the infertile north landowners granted more land for cash than in the fertile south, where they minimized land allotments but set higher values. As a result the peasants began their free life with either too great a debt or too little land. Over the years following the emancipation, the peasants underwent radically divergent experiences. Some – a small number – achieved success as independent farmers, blessed by ability, good land and good luck, the amalgamation through marriage of neighbouring plots that brought economies of scale, and so on. Others, the majority, found themselves burdened by rising taxes, increasing debt, inadequate resources and declining living standards. A middle group of indeterminate size just managed to stay afloat.

The population of Europe exploded in the second half of the nineteenth century, Russia included, with the result that the agrarian sector was heavily overpopulated. Apart from Poles and the small Jewish population of the Empire, who were largely segregated, the Russians in general did not follow the pattern of other nations of Europe who, in the late nineteenth and early twentieth century, were leaving their native lands for friendlier places or better economic opportunities. There was very little emigration from Russia proper, though some relief in pressure in the villages came from migration to the cities as factory labour, and to the sparsely populated regions of Siberia and Central Asia. Between 1896 and 1916 some two million peasants settled in these regions. But the legacy of the inequitable terms of the emancipation of 1861 was a running sore throughout the rest of the century, exercising generations of thinkers and public-spirited activists, and coming to a crisis around 1900 when there were widespread riots.

WORKERS

In Russia industrialization came late. There was a ship-building industry established by Peter the Great in his capital, St Petersburg, in the eighteenth century, when he made the first effort to modernize his vast country, but broadly speaking industry remained underdeveloped until late in the nineteenth century. Russia's entrepreneurial class was small and industrialization, while it made a good number of men rich, did not create a middle class to compare in size – let alone political influence – with those of Western Europe or the USA. The state itself was industry's main provider of capital as well as orders, especially when a great railway building programme got under way in the second half of the nineteenth century.

Russian industry was unevenly distributed geographically and employed only a comparatively small proportion of the population. Because it was the result of intensive government policy, rather than the more gradual organic path it had taken in the West, industry was characterized by very large factories, concentrating great numbers of workers who were housed, usually without their families, in barrack-like dormitories. In 1900 the number of workers employed in factories with more than twenty people and in transport and dock facilities, numbered about three million. To this may be added some fifteen million who were employed in small artisan workshops scattered through the country in cities and villages. The great majority of the population, however, remained overwhelmingly rural and agrarian, with most 'workers' still being legally classified as peasants.

Embryonic trade unions began to form in the last two decades of the century as workers sought ways to protect themselves from the excesses of factory owners. In turn the employers sought protection from a government that was eager to promote an expanding and prosperous industrial base, in which it saw the promise of social stability and imperial power. As the Marxists believed that the working class was the bearer and future beneficiary of socialist revolution, they hoped to use the workers' own organizations as a battering ram against the tsarist regime. The more intelligent workers – many of them semi-educated, thanks to student revolutionaries – resented such attempts to take over their movement and guarded it jealously. Similarly, some of the most militant Marxists, notably Lenin, rejected the idea that revolutionary organizations should be guided by the workers' movement, which they saw as narrow-minded and concerned only with small gains in the worker's lot, what Lenin called 'English trade-union consciousness', rather than the grandiose socialist revolutionary plan for sweeping away existing society altogether and rebuilding it on socialist principles.

Police harassment and manipulation, imprisonment and harsh exile to Eastern Siberia failed to dampen the workers' urge to fight for a better life, and in the years between 1900 and 1905 a rising tide of unrest, strikes and demonstrations revealed the depth of their willingness to do so.

THE INTELLIGENTSIA

Most Russian revolutionaries accepted the Marxist explanation of why socialist revolution was inevitable: the revolution would occur when society could no longer sustain the widening gap between rich and poor, capital and labour, the bourgeoisie and the proletariat, otherwise known as 'the class war'. In countries like England, the United States or Germany, where the industrial process was more advanced, the capitalist system highly developed, and personal and corporate wealth could – even with constant friction – coexist with growing labour organization, many socialists had come to see that at least a part of labour's programme could be channelled into the constitutional political process that more enlightened governments had created. They also saw that even in these more advanced countries the workers had to fight for every concession from employers, and also to endure violence and harassment at the hands of the state. They were therefore not deterred from their belief in the inevitability of a violent end to the class struggle and the eruption of socialist revolution.

In Russia there were no constitutional alternatives open to the politically conscious. Political parties were banned, along with a free press, freedom of assembly, free speech, or any of the other civil liberties enjoyed elsewhere. Political activity in Russia had always meant conspiracy, illegality and harsh penalties.

THE POLITICAL CONTEXT

Alexander II's reforms included a limited form of local self-government called the *zemstvo*, or land assembly. Both nobleman and peasant could sit on *zemstvo* boards together and the attraction this institution exerted on educated, modern-minded young Russians, who came to work as economists, agrarian experts, doctors and teachers, imported new ways of thinking and acting into the sleepy, backward Russian villages and provincial towns.

The *zemstvo* was introduced only in the central Russian provinces, as it was thought that to do so in the western (Polish) and Asian parts of the Empire would foster secessionist ideas and instability in the borderlands. Nor were its members allowed to create inter-provincial bodies, for fear they might eventually seek to establish a national legislative assembly as a rival seat of authority to that of the tsar. In fact the ultimate aim of those who supported the *zemstvo*, especially the lawyers and academics, was precisely this: many of them were inspired by the example of

11

constitutional monarchy in Britain; the more radical elements saw the kingless French Republic as a model.

The reign of Alexander II, a reforming autocrat, was bound to be contradictory. Giving a degree of autonomy with one hand, he sought with the other to restrain the energy released by reform. For conservatives, he gave too much away, for liberals, too little, and for revolutionaries he was merely an obstacle to be removed. He was finally murdered by a bomb thrown by extremists on 1 March 1881.

He was succeeded by his son, Alexander III, who was deeply conservative and now, understandably, even more defensive in his outlook. His response to the act of regicide was to greatly enlarge the security police and its powers and to clamp down on the *zemstvo*. Where his father had expanded the educational system and made it accessible to a wider cross-section of the population, Alexander III restricted admission to high schools and universities, which he saw as hotbeds of sedition. The hopes of many young people were thus blighted and they either sought an alternative in the universities of Western Europe, such as Berlin, Zurich and Paris, or they gave up the goal of self-improvement. In both cases they were instantly politicized and it was from this pool of intelligent, energetic, disappointed young people that the various strands of the large Russian revolutionary movement was formed. As the new reactionary regime included especially harsh restraints on the small Jewish population of the Empire, whose younger generation were especially keen to acquire a secular, Russian education, Jewish youth became disproportionately numerous among the revolutionaries.

The accession in 1894 of Alexander III's son, Nicholas II, was accompanied by constant and increasing tension. Depressed peasants, downtrodden workers and the frustrated politically minded all clamoured for a change in the way Russia was run and for a say in the government of the country, such as was enjoyed by the populations of more advanced European countries. The pressure for representation reached a critical point in the first years of the twentieth century when peasants were rioting, workers were striking, students were demonstrating, and when the state was fighting a senseless and disastrous war with Japan over each side's claims to Manchuria and the Korean peninsula. On 9/22 January 1905 a peaceful mass procession marched towards the tsar's palace to demand justice, only to be fired on by troops, leaving several hundred dead on the streets. Nicholas was dubbed 'Nicholas the Bloody' and his image was permanently tarnished.

In the course of 1905 practically the whole of Russian society went on to the streets to demand political reform. The tsar at last felt vulnerable, his confidence shaken. He was urged by his closest advisers to make concessions and finally in October 1905 he issued a Manifesto, conceding civil rights and the formation of a national assembly to be called the State Duma.

The war in Manchuria had been costly for Russia, both in terms of spent resources and loss of face. The biggest land empire, with the largest population, had been defeated by what the Russians had been told was an inferior Asiatic race. The difficulty of carrying large forces across 4,000 miles from the European heartland to the Far East on the incomplete Trans-Siberian Railway, and keeping them supplied with reinforcements and equipment, had been compounded by the relative ease with which the Japanese could put their troops on a land mass only two hundred miles away across the sea. The Imperial Russian Army fought bravely and well but when the Russian Fleet, which had sailed for six months halfway around the world from the Baltic to the Sea of Japan, was sunk in the course of an afternoon, the army's efforts were nullified. By the summer of 1905 Russia was ready to call a halt.

Through the good offices of the United States one

of Russia's most brilliant statesmen, the former finance minister Sergei Witte, succeeded in negotiating a peace treaty at Portsmouth, New Hampshire, that was far less punitive to Russia than might have been expected. By late 1905, with the war settled, and large new loans from Western bankers tucked away in his state coffers, Nicholas felt confident enough to water down his promises of October. The franchise for electing the State Duma turned out not to be universal but weighted in favour of the propertied classes and against the city intelligentsia and workers. Peasants, whom the government still believed to be loyal, were well represented.

THE DUMA

The single most clear demand of 1905 had been for representation, the core of the liberal philosophy. More than all other political elements, the liberals, organized as the party of Constitutional Democrats (or Kadets), valued the rule of law exemplified by the parliamentary process, and it was therefore not surprising that when the First Duma opened in 1906 it was they who held the largest bloc of seats. They were supported by peasant deputies who saw in them the *zemstvo*-inspired champions of land reform.

15

Socialists and conservatives were small elements on the left and right of this left-of-centre assembly.

The government recognized the liberals' popularity and offered ministerial posts to their leaders in a spirit of reconciliation. But it expected the liberals to condemn the use of terror as a condition for entering the government. For their part the liberals were well aware that their influence in 1905 had been fuelled by the mass rebellion of the workers and they therefore felt unable to accept the government's terms. Instead, the Duma voiced demands for universal suffrage, a general political amnesty and, above all, radical agrarian reform. The tsar regarded these demands as a challenge to his divinely anointed authority and the assembly as an affront, and he dissolved it after only two months.

This caused a split in the liberals' ranks, with the right wing entering moderate conservative parties and the rest becoming more aggressively anti-government. On the right, meanwhile, extreme militant nationalist organizations called the Black Hundreds, who foreshadowed the Fascist parties of the future, were formed in order to disrupt the political process by rousing mobs against the Jews, whom they identified as Christian Russia's enemies and the natural allies of the anti-tsarist movement in all its forms. Left-wing terrorists redoubled their efforts to achieve the same end.

The Second Duma assembled in March 1907 with a very different composition: the liberals were weakened by fragmentation, the right, the clergy, the national minorities and the revolutionary left were greatly strengthened, while the government had solid party support from the centre. The Second Duma was therefore completely unworkable and spent its days in uproar and mutual recrimination.

The government meanwhile was bent on stamping out all remaining traces of revolutionary violence in the country and established military courts to do this with summary executions – the gallows was dubbed 'Stolypin's necktie', after the tough new prime minister, Peter Stolypin – and savage sentences of imprisonment, exile and hard labour. The opposition parties demanded an amnesty and an end to the military courts and the revolutionaries threatened another revolution if the government would not give in. Instead, Stolypin advised the tsar to dissolve the Second Duma after only six weeks and in June 1907 he introduced a new electoral law which effectively bolstered the presence of right-wing and pro-government parties at the expense of the left in the Third Duma.

The period from 1907 to the outbreak of the First World War saw a sharp decline in revolutionary activity as workers tired of street politics and the government introduced some enlightened labour legislation, such as workers' insurance and factory safety regulations, and their revolutionary friends went back to their safe havens in Western Europe. There was also a growing mood of defensive nationalistic reaction in society and an open rift between the tsar and the Duma. Nicholas and, no less important, his wife, the Empress Alexandra, detested the very idea of the Duma. It had been wrung from him at his weakest moment and it embodied a denial of the autocratic principle. (Indeed, in 1906 he had resisted issuing a constitution because of its republican overtones and had insisted that Russia's new political framework be described as 'Fundamental Laws'.)

RASPUTIN

One figure that greatly worsened relations in the Third Duma was Rasputin. Shortly after the empress gave birth to a son in 1904, having first produced four daughters, it was discovered that the boy suffered from haemophilia, a blood disorder carried by female descendants of Queen Victoria and transmitted to male offspring. No cure was available but in 1905 Gregory Rasputin, a 'holy man' from Siberia who was alleged to have healing powers, was introduced to the royal family and, indeed, was able to alleviate the boy's pain and stop his bleeding by inducing a feeling of relaxation and confidence. Modern medical opinion confirms that this approach can have beneficial effects.

The empress, a deeply religious and rather unworldly woman, was uneasy at court, where she knew her husband was held in disdain by his mother and her circle for his lack of statesmanlike qualities. She confined herself increasingly to the palace at Tsarskoe Selo outside St Petersburg and concentrated her efforts on the well-being of her family, especially her afflicted son, Alexei, the tsarevich and heir to the throne of Russia. Once it was clear that Rasputin had a beneficial effect on the tsarevich, Alexandra put her trust in him and would hear nothing said against him by those who saw that placing a wild and unpredictable wanderer from Siberia in the very bosom of the royal family was to create a potential danger to the standing and image of the Romanov dynasty itself.

Rasputin had been introduced to the tsar's family

and to St Petersburg society through his connections in the church, where he enjoyed the patronage of senior dignitaries. But he was a complex figure. Far from devoting himself to a life of prayer and contemplation, he was a lecherous gourmandizing libertine who exploited his connections to gain easy access to high society, where he enjoyed the scandalous attention of women, whether they were the wives and daughters of aristocrats and ministers, or prostitutes whom he picked up in the public baths, or took with him to hear gypsy music in the capital's best nightspots. He also made useful friends with men in high finance, who did both him and themselves favours by the relationship. He was, in short, highly disreputable and potentially lethal to the image of the Romanov family.

In April 1912 Alexander Guchkov, the Speaker of the Duma and leader of the moderate Octobrist Party, openly attacked the royal couple for harbouring Rasputin. He may even have been responsible for circulating copies of stolen letters from the empress to Rasputin in which some of her remarks could be misconstrued as signs of intimacy. It was not until this moment, however, that the public was made aware of the tsarevich's illness. He was thought to be dying of yet another haemorrhage and the tsar released an appeal for national prayers to be said, giving the reason. In the event it was Rasputin's prayers, and a telegram he sent from Siberia, that were credited by the empress for the boy's survival. In their ignorance the public had hitherto entertained quite different thoughts: there were four young princesses and the empress herself to feed the prurient rumours that had begun circulating at this time and that Rasputin's scandalous behaviour in public did nothing to curtail. Guchkov's attack was doubly painful to the royal couple: he advertised himself as a loyal subject but showed no sensitivity to the private tragedy being endured by Nicholas and Alexandra. His campaign earned him their enduring hatred.

This conflict was important for two reasons: first, it foreshadowed a far more serious clash that would occur during the war, and second, as with all other debates in the Duma, it was reported in the press, and thus led to the erosion of the tsar's personal image. The press in Russia had mushroomed after 1905 when censorship rules were relaxed. The detailed reporting of speeches in the Duma, attacking both the government and the tsar personally, assumed enormous significance. The Russian people had never seen their monarch so

21

openly criticized. The idea that he was human – indeed, rumours that he was also partial to the vodka bottle made him all too human in the eyes of the Russian public – undermined the dogma that he ruled by divine right or that he could cure Russia's ills, were it not for his wrong-headed or malevolent ministers. The notion that the tsar himself might be responsible for Russia's problems began to take root.

Weak-willed and easily influenced by persuasive advisors, Nicholas was a man of ordinary intelligence and little training for the job, and he was happiest when ensconced with his loving family rather than dealing with ministers and having to face the growing ambitions of the Duma. Equally, he had a stubborn streak and could act impulsively in a, usually vain, effort to show strength of character. He was especially susceptible to his wife's insistence that he act like an autocrat and show who was master. She, meanwhile, was highly susceptible to Rasputin's suggestions about which ministers to advance and which ones to set aside in the government, and their relationship, while merely scandalous in peacetime, became a positive threat to the regime when it came under the stress of full-scale modern war.

TWO

War

The relative calm, often described as 'drift', in the years following the crushing of the 1905 revolution was disturbed in 1912 by the particularly bloody suppression of a strike by gold miners on the Lena river in Western Siberia. To describe what ensued as a 'revolutionary upsurge', as Soviet historians claimed, is to exaggerate, but for the next two years Russian workers regained a good measure of their earlier militancy, which was now also fuelled by the inflammatory speeches of the Duma opposition, the press coverage of the Rasputin scandal and corruption in government circles.

Yet, when Russia entered the war in August 1914, the public mood changed abruptly to one of excited patriotism. The annual call-up of conscripts had in the past invariably been accompanied by local acts of resistance, self-mutilation and drunken disorderliness. Now in 1914 the mobilization got under way with extraordinary efficiency. A wave of anti-German feeling swept the country, the German embassy was burnt down by a large angry mob, and the tsar authorized the change of the capital's name from the German-sounding Sankt Peterburg to its Slavonic equivalent, Petrograd.

The Duma had been in recess when war was declared. At a one-day session on 8 August the deputies staged a patriotic demonstration. Only the Social Democrats, for once united, condemned the war and refused to vote for war credits – the only socialists in the Socialist International to do so. But the tsar believed that the sacred task of conducting the war effort should be in the hands of those who knew their responsibilities to the fatherland, that is, his own appointees, not 'power-hungry' politicians. He suspended the Duma for six months and, with the advice of his Council of Ministers only, personally issued a spate of emergency legislation by decree.

Never cordial, relations between the regime and the leaders of the opposition were now openly distrustful. By the middle of 1915, however, the public mood had changed dramatically. Crushing defeats of the Imperial Russian Army in the opening campaigns took a heavy toll on morale, to say nothing of the reputation of the military leadership which desperately searched for scapegoats. The war minister was dismissed in disgrace and a senior officer was executed on trumped-up charges of spying for the Germans, as spy mania seized the public imagination.

In the western provinces, where the main campaigns were taking place, and where the population was predominantly Polish, Lithuanian and Jewish, the Jews were singled out as a major cause of Russia's woes. As Russian Jews mostly spoke Yiddish, which derives from medieval German, it was easy to issue a general accusation of collaboration with the enemy, and many were hanged by the military authorities after summary court martial. Hundreds of thousands of Jews were given twenty-four hours notice to leave their homes and to move as refugees further east into the Russian interior on the spurious grounds that they were being evacuated for their own safety. Roads and rail transport, already overloaded with military traffic, now became choked with this additional burden, only adding to the hostility towards a minority that had been reviled for generations.

The plight of the Russian Jews became an international scandal at the same time as the tsar was being urged by his closest adviser, his wife, with Rasputin's backing, to replace his uncle, the Grand Duke Nikolai Nikolayevich, as Commander-in-Chief, and to take over the post himself. This would have the effect of appeasing Allied opinion, especially that of Great Britain, and also of removing from the scene a figure whose military skills were deeply flawed and his political ambition supposedly insatiable. He was sent with his rabidly anti-Semitic chief of staff, General Yanushkevich, to the Caucasian Front. For the first and probably the only time in his life, Nicholas felt like the autocrat he, and his wife, thought he ought to be.

THE PATH TO FEBRUARY

Many of his more enlightened officials were concerned that, by removing himself to the General Headquarters and leaving his wife to hold the balance between his ministers, to interview candidates for senior posts and make her recommendations to her husband, the tsar had concocted a recipe for potential disaster. Knowing that the empress was so completely under the spell of Rasputin, to whom she referred in her letters to her husband as 'Our Friend', it was feared, prophetically, that the administration would become chaotic and subject to caprice. For his part Nicholas thought his wife ideal for the role. He wrote to her, shortly after leaving for GHQ: 'What a pity that you have not been fulfilling this duty [until now].'[1]

A good minister in Alexandra's view was one who met with Rasputin's approval and had no mind of his own. She was especially incensed by the ministers who had opposed the tsar's assumption of supreme command – 'I long to thrash nearly all of them'[2] – and in the course of 1915 to 1916 she got rid of seven of the original ten.

Born Princess Alix of Hesse-Darmstadt, and now dubbed 'the German woman', the empress became the object of nonsensical rumours about a separate peace with Germany, which she was allegedly negotiating through her German relatives. The intimacy Rasputin was thought to enjoy in her company spawned further rumours of breaches in state security. In reality, whenever the tsar wrote to her on military affairs, he urged her always to 'keep it to *yourself*'. And in September 1916, when she sent her husband a long account of Rasputin's views on some important matters of state, including the names of new ministerial candidates, the tsar replied, 'Our Friend's opinions of people are sometimes very strange, as you know yourself – therefore one must be careful, especially with appointments to high office'.

When Nicholas took over as Commander-in-Chief in September 1915 he thought it prudent at last to bow to pressure by allowing leading industrialists and politicians to form committees to supervise the conversion of Russian industry to war production. The chairman of the Central War Industries Committee was Alexander Guchkov, the empress's sworn enemy. A nationwide network of powerful public figures, many of them holding interlocking company directorships, emerged and was also connected with the political Free Masons in Petrograd and Moscow, who included leading politicians from a broad spectrum of parties from left to right. The empress regarded these men as usurpers of the royal prerogative. She wrote to Nicholas that she would like to see Guchkov hanged and the War Industries Committee closed down.

Instead the Duma was recalled and a campaign for including public figures in the government – 'a government enjoying public confidence' – gathered momentum. About 300 deputies, ranging from Kadets to moderate nationalists, formed a united front that came to be known as the Progressive Bloc. Its primary aim was to heal the rift with the government and facilitate the effective conduct of the war.

Thanks to the efforts of the network administered

by the Central War Industries Committee, industry was put on a war footing. Increasingly close cooperation with the military leadership, as well as improved production by the state sector, generated rising morale, as well as performance. In the summer of 1916 the army gained an impressive victory under General Brusilov and, by the end of 1916, with the supply position greatly improved, morale rose even higher. It was, however, short-lived. Brusilov's success proved to be of comparatively little strategic significance and the rift between the tsar and the opposition opened still wider.

Throughout 1916 the 'ministerial leapfrog', of which even the tsar complained to his wife, went on as one vain incompetent official after another was advanced by the empress, replacing either a more high-minded rival or an equally venal competitor who had offended her sensibilities. In January 1916, with extraordinary lack of tact, she had replaced the geriatric prime minister, Goremykin, with a known corrupt and sycophantic bureaucrat, whose German name, Stuermer, only intensified the rumours that she was guided by 'dark forces' and seeking to serve German interests at the expense of her adopted country. Stuermer's appointment enraged even extreme conservatives, while the Allied military representatives in Russia despaired. The Progressive Bloc was exasperated and condemnation of the alleged influence of Rasputin on the most important decisions being made by the government became widespread in Petrograd. By the winter, with the memory of Brusilov's glory already faded, a real sense of political crisis existed.

This was exacerbated by the worsening dislocation of the rear. The army's insatiable appetite for men, ammunition, food and transport was more than the domestic economy could stand without suffering acute shortage and disruption itself. The pressure was felt most acutely where it mattered most, namely in the capital, Petrograd, the country's most industrialized city and the focus of the most sensitive political activity. There was fear that food and fuel would be in short supply in the coming winter.

When the Duma reconvened on 14 November 1916, few deputies were prepared to continue cooperating with the government. In a long speech the moderate Kadet leader, Paul Milyukov (a university professor of history), described Russia's situation as that of a country led in war by a gang of incompetents whose mistakes and ineptitude were due either to stupidity or treason. He reminded deputies that the government was claiming that to organize the rear for war, as the Duma wanted, would mean organizing the revolution. The government, he said, 'consciously prefers chaos . . . what is that, stupidity or treason?'[3]

Encapsulating the long campaign the opposition had conducted against the empress and Rasputin, Milyukov's indictment of the regime was printed in thousands of copies and distributed widely, including to the front. Rumours flew in the capital about plots to murder Rasputin and the 'holy man' himself, in a remarkably prophetic letter to the tsar, predicted his own imminent death and the immersion of Russia in a bloodbath.

Among those who heard Milyukov deliver his speech was Prince Felix Yusupov, the husband of one of the tsar's nieces, and heir of the richest family in Russia. Already consumed by hatred for Rasputin for complex personal reasons, as well as for the danger he posed to the monarchy, Yusupov quickly found a group of like-minded men who would join him in a conspiracy to murder the empress's spiritual adviser. They included Grand Duke Dmitri Pavlovich, who was a nephew of the tsar, Vladimir Purishkevich, a notoriously controversial right-wing deputy, Lieutenant Ivan Sukhotin, a young friend of Yusupov's, and a physician, Dr Stanislaus Lazovert.

On 29 December Rasputin was lured to Yusupov's palatial residence in Petrograd, and, after poisoning, shooting, savage beating and, possibly, castration, he was rolled up in a carpet and stuffed through a hole in the ice in the Neva river. His body was discovered three days later and a post-mortem showed that water in his lungs suggested he had survived all his assassins' efforts and died from drowning.

Whether because it occurred too late, or demonstrated that his influence had been exaggerated, the murder of Rasputin did nothing to change the political situation. The empress was devastated by the loss of her indispensable 'Friend' but the tsar still resisted the appeals of leading figures to give them authority.

The Duma was adjourned and the Progressive Bloc now planned a more drastic solution, namely, the abdication of Nicholas in favour of his son, with his brother, Grand Duke Michael, taking over as regent. Picking up the militant tone of the Duma, the Labour Group in the Central War Industries Committee called on the workers of the capital to demonstrate on the day the Duma was due to reassemble. However, the Group was arrested in late January and, because of disagreements between the Bolsheviks and Mensheviks, the demonstration did not take place.

The Duma was recalled on 12 March (NS) in an atmosphere of total crisis. A native of Lenin's birthplace and whose father had been the young Lenin's headmaster, Alexander Kerensky, the leader of the Labour-Socialist Revolutionary group on the Duma, and a member of the cross-party inner circle of the Progressive Bloc, told an agitated assembly that it was time to get rid of the tsar, by assassination if necessary. But no action was taken, either by the opposition to further this plan, or by the government to suppress its instigator.

THREE

The February/March Revolution

The eruption occurred on 8 March. A bakers' strike led to disturbances in bread queues which quickly spread to the centre and the industrial suburbs. It coincided with the celebration of International Women's Day and was joined by workers from the huge Putilov armaments factory whose militancy increased the tension. When it emerged that the capital had only three days' supply of flour, the meetings turned into an anti-government riot. By the next day huge strikes were taking place, with organized efforts to carry the demonstration into the city centre. Cossack detachments, who were the traditional scourge of street protests, refrained from taking any action and even appeared to be on the side of the crowds. By 10 March the city was in the grip of a general strike.

The capital also harboured as many as 200,000 troops, many of them new recruits or old hands convalescing from the trenches, neither group a reliable source of support for the government, and both affected by revolutionary agitation. Mutiny broke out in one company on the evening of the 11th and by the next morning almost the entire garrison was in revolt. On 12 March the situation reached its crisis, as thousands of strikers again crowded into the streets and were now joined by armed troops who had 'gone over to the revolution'. They occupied the city's chief prison, the Peter-Paul Fortress, and released prisoners from gaol, including the Labour Group of the War Industries Committee. When Nicholas II was informed of the position, he ordered the military commandant to 'suppress all disorders in the capital tomorrow, as they are intolerable at this time of war with Germany and Austria'.[1]

On the same day the Duma openly defied the tsar's order of the previous day to adjourn and established a Provisional Committee whose task was to deal with the desperate conditions in the capital: the prospect of total breakdown in production and army discipline threatened far worse than the almost forgotten war.

By 13 March the tsarist government lost all authority, its members either arrested or hiding at home. The tsar, finally realizing the seriousness of the situation, left GHQ at Mogilev for the capital on the morning of that day but was advised to divert his train to Northern HQ at Pskov, as the line was occupied by revolutionary troops. He was met at Pskov by his senior generals who begged him to grant a constitution and a representative government. Still believing a constitutional monarchy to be a possibility, he sent a cable to the President of the Duma, Fedor Rodzianko, giving him permission to form a government. The Provisional Committee also believed a constitutional monarchy was the best option, as long as the country was at war, and on 15 March sent Alexander Guchkov and Vasili Shulgin, a right-wing deputy, to the tsar with the task of persuading Nicholas to abdicate in favour of his son, with his brother, Grand Duke Michael, as regent.

The failure of any of his senior officers to come to the tsar's support must have played a crucial part in his decision to abdicate. For them he had become a lame-duck emperor, an inadequate military commander, a dead weight that they had been carrying out of a redundant sense of loyalty, and that was undermining their task of fighting the war to a victorious conclusion. They had come to see that military victory lay with the Duma and its industrial backers, rather than in a fumbling isolated tsar.

Faced with a hopeless situation that he was powerless to alter, Nicholas abdicated in favour of his brother, Michael, rather than his sickly son. Back in the capital, however, when Michael was told by the republican-minded Kerensky that the new revolutionary government could not guarantee his personal safety, the Grand Duke – who had democratic sympathies – declined the crown. The 300-year-old Romanov dynasty slipped into history virtually by default: monarchists had returned from GHQ to the capital with the offer of a new tsar; republicans had frightened the successor into handing over to a new republican regime.

Also on 12 March left-wing deputies, trade union leaders and the released members of the Labour Group formed a Provisional Executive Committee of the Soviet (Council) of Workers' Deputies. The first Soviet had been organized in the 1905 revolution as a form of alternative workers' government, with the fiery Leon Trotsky as its most prominent figure. Trotsky, or Lev Bronstein to give him his real name, was born in 1879 in Southern Russia, the son of a Jewish small farmer. Like so many of his comrades in the revolutionary movement, he had a turbulent youth which included expulsion from university, imprisonment and deportation to exile in Siberia – and multiple escapes. He met Lenin in London in 1902 and became a close associate, breaking with him the following year when the Social Democrats split into Bolshevik and Menshevik wings. Trotsky came to occupy a position somewhere between the two, reflecting his independent character rather than serious ideological differences.

The Petrograd Soviet of 1917 was established in conscious emulation of that heroic enterprise. As the Duma was the focus of public attention, the Soviet established its headquarters in the same building as the Duma Committee, the Tauride Palace. Recognizing the large presence of armed soldiers among the crowds that mobbed its first meeting, the Soviet renamed itself the Soviet of Workers' and Soldiers' Deputies – adding Peasants' in due course – and set about dealing with the food and fuel shortages that had precipitated the crisis. Its aims were at first to protect its constituents' interests and to give the new government support in the war, providing it did not pursue offensive action. On 15 March the Soviet published its Order No. 1, calling for soldiers' committees to be set up in every unit and the abolition of hierarchical relations between officers and men. With the breakdown in military discipline now assured, desertions, fraternization with the enemy and refusal to fight anything but a defensive war in order to achieve a 'democratic peace' without 'annexations or reparations' became widespread.

SOCIALISTS AND THE WAR

While most European socialist parties had supported the war since mobilization in August 1914, the Russians, whether Bolshevik or Menshevik, had split into a number of groupings, some in favour of fighting to a victorious end, others adopting a defensist position. In 1915 a radical group of European socialists, meeting in the Swiss village of Zimmerwald, had called for immediate peace. A 'Left Zimmerwald' faction argued for turning the imperialist war into civil war, in which the worker-peasant soldiers must turn their rifles on their class enemies, the officer corps, and thus launch the socialist revolution on an international scale. This group was led by Vladimir Lenin who, since the outbreak of the war, had been urging that a Russian defeat was not only a 'lesser evil' than a German victory but was also the best possible setting for revolution.

The Duma's attacks on the tsar had been prompted by the failings of the Imperial Russian Army and it was clear therefore that the new regime was committed to pursuing the war effort more effectively. To the ordinary soldier, however, the departure of the tsar signalled the end of the war and it was with the greatest difficulty thereafter that the Provisional Government was able to make them fight. Soldiers' deputies in the Soviet ensured that maximum pressure was maintained on the government to relinquish any aggressive intentions. The Soviet, in other words, tacitly supported the new regime but made it plain that the Provisional Government must negotiate an early end to the war.

This position was adopted even by such members of the Bolshevik Central Committee as Stalin and Kamenev, who returned from exile in Siberia with the overthrow of the tsar, seemingly oblivious of their leader's exhortations from Switzerland not to give the slightest credence to the liberal government and its friends. Joseph Stalin (real name Dzhugashvili), the son of an impoverished Georgian bootmaker, had risen rapidly from provincial obscurity to the Central Committee after organizing bank robberies in his native Georgia to help fill the coffers of the Bolshevik Party in 1905. Lev Kamenev

41

was also an important member of the Bolshevik leadership after 1905, notably in its press activities.

From its outbreak Lenin had publicly argued that the war was an imperialistic evil that would benefit only international capital, while sacrificing the workers of the belligerent countries. Since such anti-war propaganda was effectively censored in Russia, where many Bolsheviks who voiced it were sent away to Siberia for long periods of exile, the message had very little impact. Nor did it penetrate very deep in the other countries at war, however appealing it might have seemed to those being sacrificed. Patriotic propaganda, and the means to deliver it, had never been stronger, and campaigns against the war, such as conscientious objection or strikes in munitions factories, never became popular or widespread.

One of the most potentially powerful propaganda weapons to be used against the imperial powers was that of national self-determination. Soon after its inception in 1903 the Russian Social Democratic Party had rejected any form of nationalism in its programme in the belief that socialist revolution would sweep away all forms of discrimination, including national or ethnic. The issue had acquired some urgency since the emergence of a relatively strong separate organization of Jewish workers and intellectuals had threatened to undermine the unity of the main party, which many Jewish revolutionaries found preferable to an ethnically closed membership. In due course, however, the Mensheviks came to see the progressive part that could be played by the separately organized workers of the national minorities, such as the Latvians, Armenians, Ukrainians, Georgians, Poles and Jews, and incorporated national-cultural autonomy into their programme and practice.

The Bolsheviks, dominated by Lenin, accepted that national self-determination had an appeal across the spectrum of ethnic minorities in the Russian Empire but steadfastly opposed giving active support to such a platform. They believed that nationalism, like religion, acted like a drug on the workers' class consciousness and that its separatism was an affront to the Marxist slogan, 'Workers of the world unite!' The rampant nationalism of wartime only confirmed them in this view, for it had led workers of different countries to obey the orders of their bourgeois officers to slaughter brother workers from other countries.

But the war also led Lenin to revise this view. Much to the disgust of some of his more left-wing comrades, such as Nikolai Bukharin, by 1915 Lenin was advocating the revolutionary potential of national movements in the multinational armies of both sides. The Russian Empire, he believed, was particularly vulnerable, and he was prepared to go to any lengths to undermine the possibility of a Russian victory. Bukharin had made the mistake of thinking that Lenin had altered his view in principle, whereas Lenin was a consummate and ruthless revolutionary who would contort and reshape his ideas into the most appropriate weapons to achieve his goal of socialist power. He claimed that Marxists were indifferent as to who won the war. They should let the capitalist dogs eat each other while he led the workers into a position to seize power where the ruling dog was weakest, i.e. Russia.

The German government, meanwhile, had been expecting that the fall of the tsar would knock Russia out of the war and allow its forces to concentrate on the Western Front alone. Instead, in March 1917, it faced a new regime in Russia committed to continuing the war to victory. It therefore welcomed an idea, originated by a maverick Russian social democrat revolutionary called Alexander Helphand-Parvus, and raised by its military intelligence service, to facilitate Lenin's return from Switzerland back to Petrograd, via Germany and Scandinavia, and to introduce him 'like a revolutionary bacillus' (Churchill's words) into the political crucible.

Lenin was met at the station in Petrograd on 3/16 April 1917 by Menshevik leaders from the Soviet who told him that they expected him to join them in defending the achievements of the revolution. Ignoring them, he turned to the crowd of soldiers and workers and proclaimed that the German workers, i.e. soldiers, were about to turn their rifles on their capitalist exploiters. 'The Russian revolution, achieved by you, has opened a new epoch.'[2]

THE DUAL POWER

Despite the fact that the new revolutionary Provisional Government was headed at first by the inappropriately named Prince Lvov, it was true to its liberal and democratic credentials and introduced full civil and political equality for all the peoples of the multinational former empire. But its eight-month rule was bedevilled by a dilemma: it was unwilling to abandon its democratic Allies, Britain and France, by making a separate peace with Germany; and it was unwilling, until the war was over, to convene a Constituent Assembly whose task would be to determine Russia's constitutional form. Composed of the elected representatives of the people, the Provisional Government had authority but little power, which it reflected in the name it chose for itself.

The Petrograd Soviet, on the other hand, claiming to be the voice of the 'people', had considerable power at its command, if it chose to exercise it, but lacked legitimate authority. The period from February to October was dominated therefore by constant conflict and tension between the Provisional Government and the Soviet and came to be known as the Dual Power.

The Soviet, meanwhile, had problems of its own. As a coalition of broadly socialist forces it soon acquired a left wing, represented by Lenin's Bolsheviks and their various internationalist fellow-travellers; it also acquired a right wing divided between those Mensheviks who still argued for the defence of the country and those who adopted the most popular socialist slogan, 'immediate peace without annexations or reparations'. In general the moderate socialists felt that the new liberal regime must be given time to mature, before any more precipitous move towards socialist revolution was undertaken.

Once Lenin had dragooned his party into accepting his uncompromising stand against collaboration with the new regime, taking about one month to do so, the Bolsheviks pursued an aggressive policy of agitation among the front-line troops. The Soviet had already instigated the formation of soldiers' committees at the front and in the garrisons and charged them with monitoring the 'revolutionary correctness' of military orders, thus making a mockery of the line of command and, indeed, on many occasions taking matters as far as mob rule and lynching.

Since 1915 the German High Command had been in secret contact with Alexander Helphand. He had played an influential role in the 1905 revolution when, as a close comrade of Trotsky, he had palpably exacerbated the situation by calling for the non-payment of taxes to bring down the government. He had then gone to work as a journalist in Turkey, supporting the Young Turk movement, and in 1915 had established an institute in Copenhagen, ostensibly to study the social consequences of the war. His real concerns were two-fold: one, to raise large sums of money from a range of nefarious trading operations through Scandinavia to Russia, and two, to engage the German government in a plan to undermine the

Russian war effort by supporting the Bolsheviks. Once the Germans realized that the Provisional Government had no intention of withdrawing from the war, they applied Parvus's plan with vigour. They called it their 'Revolutionary Policy'.

Bolshevik support undulated during the summer of 1917 as rumours of Lenin's dealings with the Germans overshadowed, or were overshadowed by, the ebb and flow of deserters and the government's efforts to deal with them. At the First Congress of Soviets, which took place in Petrograd in June, the delegates lamented the lack of leadership and argued that only a coalition could govern Russia, as no single party could do so alone. To the incredulous mirth of the other delegates present Lenin jumped up and declared, 'Yes, there is!' Nobody could imagine that the Bolsheviks and their maverick leader could possibly rule the country in its present state of extreme need.

The Mensheviks were exhibiting a profound hesitancy. They rejected the idea of seizing power before the programme of the February Revolution had been played out, before, that is, the workers showed they were capable of holding power for themselves. Like the liberals they feared that just beneath the veneer of their social democratic convictions, the Russian workers were still a primitive force that could, if power was thrust on them, wreck the chances of a liberal democracy. Their political will was thus paralyzed and they were rendered incapable of taking power, even when the crowds were urging them to do so. In the meantime the middle classes waited in trepidation as the mobs on the streets expressed growing hostility against the *burzhui* (bourgeois).

The secret funding from Germany meanwhile enabled the Bolsheviks to print a wide range of leaflets, calling on the troops to leave their posts and to fraternize with the Germans – in other words to end the war. The government tried to stifle this activity by assembling evidence to indict Lenin as a German agent. The case was close to completion in July, when Lenin decided that it was time to make a bid for power. The Bolsheviks rallied their military and other supporters and staged a mass demonstration in the capital. They proposed no specific demands and ostensibly the mass meeting was not a Bolshevik event, as such: rather a show of popular strength with the aim of letting the Provisional Government know where the real power lay.

In fact, without an expressed cause, the demonstration was easily dispersed by loyal forces. At the same moment rumours of Lenin's German connection were circulated, bringing down on his head loud condemnation from the very masses he had been counting on. Kerensky was literally on the point of having Lenin arrested and put on trial, when Lenin was tipped off. He managed to escape, in disguise, to neighbouring Finland.

FOUR

OCTOBER

The officer corps had been demoralized by the tsar's abdication. He had after all been their Commander-in-Chief and for him to leave his post in the middle of the hardest war Russia had ever fought, and seemed to be losing, was in the eyes of many officers tantamount to treason. For most ordinary soldiers the departure of the tsar was virtually synonymous with the end of the war itself: was it not *his* war they had been fighting?

The population at large greeted the event as a turning-point, not only in the war but in Russian history. Euphorically they welcomed the change as an important sign of a new beginning, and most expected the new regime to reinvigorate the war effort. Those who actively wanted and worked for Russia to be defeated were the apparently insignificant handful of Leninists who had followed their leader's line since the Zimmerwald Conference of 1915. Ordinary Russians hoped that the war would end in a Russian victory, or at least not an ignominious defeat, and the tsar's abject failure to lead his army to success had been one of the main factors leading to his overthrow. As they watched their troops becoming daily more mutinous, however, deserting *en masse* and flocking to the Bolsheviks who were telling them not to fight, the population became increasingly pessimistic.

Russia in the summer of 1917 was a country without leaders – 'the freest country in the world', as Lenin called it. The ravages of war on the economy had created rampant inflation and the drastic devaluation of the currency. Even before February there had been several large-scale strikes on purely economic issues and now, after the euphoria that accompanied the end of the Romanov dynasty died down, life was hard and getting harder.

The railways, which had been overloaded with military and civilian traffic before February, became increasingly dislocated throughout 1917 as refugees and deserters fought for space in the scramble to find a safe haven. Law and order were now a thing of the past as Provisional Government officials strove in vain to exercise their tenuous and dwindling authority. Public services in the capitals, Petrograd and Moscow, continued to function to some extent, with the trams running and the telephones working, but food and fuel supplies were becoming increasingly unreliable and the prospect of winter in such conditions only added to the universal feeling of insecurity.

The country was also mired in the most profound chaos and disorder. As discipline broke down in the army, as the soldiers 'voted with their feet' and deserted the trenches in their tens of thousands, so the cities away from the war zone in the west were crowded with disoriented, desperate, armed men. In emulation of the two capitals mass meetings were taking place in all the provincial capitals, from Riga on the Baltic Sea to Vladivostok on the Pacific coast, Soviets were springing up and workers and peasants and their brothers-in-uniform were passing ever more radical resolutions, finding in the Bolsheviks the sole political party that openly encouraged desertion and promised salvation.

THE KORNILOV MOVEMENT

Indignation and frustration at Russia's plight was felt most acutely by the officer corps and it was best expressed by no less a figure than the Supreme

Commander, General Lavr Kornilov. The son of a Cossack father and Tartar mother, Kornilov had the appearance of an Asiatic chieftain. A talent for Asiatic languages had qualified him for service as an undercover military intelligence agent in Iran and India and he had had a distinguished fighting record in campaigns in the Russo-Japanese War.

As a military man, Kornilov regarded himself as loyal to the ideals of February – he described himself as a 'son of the revolution' – and he wanted the government, under Alexander Kerensky, to act more vigorously in the defence of those ideals. He looked to his prime minister to take a tough line over the Bolsheviks' agitation and the desertion it was provoking. He had seen the line of command crumble in the army, most critically at the front, where the Soldiers' Committees which sprang up in emulation of workers' Soviets scrutinized and discussed their officers' orders in order to judge their 'political correctness', i.e. the degree to which they conformed to the line dictated by the Petrograd Soviet.

While Kornilov had no objection in principle to the idea of soldiers' organizations, he drew the line at insubordination and was incensed by what the troops were able to read in the copies of Lenin's

Trench Pravda that circulated at the front. He wanted discipline restored, respect for commanders and, most controversially, the restoration of the death penalty for desertion, which the Provisional Government had abolished in March in its post-revolutionary liberal euphoria. Without sanctions, including the extreme sanction, Kornilov argued, the army faced defeat. He believed that the fount of all the disorder in the army was in the Petrograd Soviet and he urged his prime minister to take a tougher line with that body.

Although a revolutionary by affiliation Kerensky had a strong streak of liberal respect for fairness, and was uneasy about suppressing what he saw as the legitimate, if disruptive, organization of the workers' and soldiers' deputies, even if it was plainly the Bolsheviks who were raising the revolutionary temper of the armed mobs. He therefore hesitated over Kornilov's exhortation to crush the Petrograd Soviet and bring back discipline in the army by reinstating the death penalty.

In a confused exchange by special telegraph in late August Kerensky conveyed the impression that he was in agreement with Kornilov's proposal to send a detachment of loyal crack troops to the capital to disperse the Soviet. But Kerensky, nominally a Socialist Revolutionary but by now, as prime minister, seriously divided in his loyalties, became suspicious that Kornilov might also use the opportunity to get rid of him too, and he therefore ordered the rampant general to call the operation off.

Kornilov chose to ignore or misunderstand his chief's order and pressed on regardless towards the capital. In a panic Kerensky armed the Soviet and its supporters and called on them to 'defend the revolution'. In the event the Kornilov operation petered out as workers and rebellious troops along the route taken by his forces persuaded his troops to join them or to turn back. Kornilov was arrested and the officer corps was now utterly alienated.

THE BOLSHEVIK COUP

Lenin, who had gone into hiding in Finland since the collapse of his bid for power in July, kept up a steady flow of frantic letters to his lieutenants in the capital, urging them that the time for revolution was ripe and that they must organize an immediate armed uprising and seize the power which, in Trotsky's words, was lying abandoned on the streets. He returned to the capital in secret in late October and held a meeting with twelve of the twenty-one members of the Central Committee. After long and heated debate, he managed to persuade ten of those present that if they did not seize the moment it would pass – perhaps forever.

Whatever the future consequences of this attitude, in purely practical terms Lenin was right to assert that the time to pounce had come. If the Bolshevik Party was ever to come into power, the time was now. The Provisional Government was impotent, the army was virtually leaderless and disintegrating rapidly, and in his ineptitude over the Kornilov affair Kerensky had deprived his administration of any semblance of serious military support. After the Kornilov fiasco there were as many as 40,000 assorted armed men, called Red Guards, under Bolshevik command in Petrograd.

Trotsky, as the chairman of the Petrograd Soviet, formed a Revolutionary Military Council and made his preparations. He was aware, however, that if the Bolsheviks succeeded in their bid to seize power in their own name, there was no assurance that they would have the support of all the workers and soldiers in Petrograd, let alone the country at large, where it was the Soviets that expressed their interests on a non-party basis. To seize power for a single party, namely, the Bolshevik Party, risked losing power in the Soviets. He therefore urged Lenin to plan the uprising to coincide with the forthcoming Second Congress of Soviets, thus enabling the Bolsheviks to claim that power had been transferred to the people's representatives, the Soviet Deputies.

Not all the Bolshevik leaders were confident that an uprising would succeed or even that it was desirable that it should. They were unsure about the level of support to expect and also wondered if they themselves were capable of governing, let alone extracting Russia painlessly from the war.

Two of the leading figures in the Central Committee, Lev Kamenev and Gregory Zinoviev – the latter having just spent the summer in hiding with Lenin – took the line that the Party should concentrate on consolidating its support in the Soviets and also await the elections planned for the forthcoming Constituent Assembly where, they believed, they would receive a majority that reflected their general strength. The Provisional Government had organized these elections on a universal and fully democratic franchise – due at first to take place in September and then delayed until November – and had justified its procrastination on many important areas of new legislation and reform by urging the public to wait for the Constituent Assembly as the supreme arbiter, the voice of the people. The Bolshevik waverers, Kamenev and Zinoviev, were out-voted ten to two and Lenin's decision to seize power was accepted.

The Second Congress of Soviets duly took place on 25 October/7 November. Its main purpose was to debate the question of how to replace the Provisional Government with a Soviet Government. But that very night the Bolsheviks seized power. On the signal of a blank shell-shot from the cruiser *Aurora*, which lay at anchor on the Neva river opposite the Winter Palace – a live shell would have caused far more damage than the pockmarks caused by rifle fire – they overcame what little resistance government forces could put up; key positions in the city, such as the main post and telegraph office and the railways stations, were occupied by Red Guards, who also swept into the Winter Palace and arrested the Provisional Government. Kerensky escaped in disguise with the vain intention of raising a force to restore his regime.

When Trotsky announced that power had been seized in the name of the Soviets, the Mensheviks, along with other groups of moderate socialists, were outraged. They had long and bitter experience of

Lenin's Machiavellian methods and were not taken in by the mendacious claim that power was now in the hands of the Soviets. They declared that they would not remain among such criminals. The chairman, Kamenev, urged them to stay but Trotsky called out in contempt: ' . . . let them go. They are just so much refuse which will be swept into the garbage heap of history!'[1]

FIVE

Civil War

The Bolshevik coup was presented as the coming to power of the Soviets of Workers', Soldiers' and Peasants' Deputies, and all the new state institutions created by Lenin and his party were labelled to conform to this version. Lenin's cabinet was called the Sovnarkom, or Soviet of People's Commissars – Trotsky and Lenin together devised this title for ministers in a moment of ironic deference to the French Revolution – and all national, regional and local government bodies became Soviets. The country itself was renamed the Soviet Republic and in 1922 the Soviet Union. Yet from its inception until its demise in 1991 the state was governed by the Bolshevik Party, renamed in 1918 as the Communist Party, which, through its supreme body, the Politburo, originated and sanctioned all policy making, and through a strictly hierarchical pyramidal structure controlled every aspect of political, economic, social, cultural and intellectual life of the country.

The purpose of the Russian revolution – both according to the Marxist scheme and Lenin's intentions – had been to transform the entire culture of the society, to make it work-oriented, free of economic and all other forms of exploitation and discrimination. To achieve these goals the Bolsheviks set about destroying the middle classes, which they identified as the bearers of capitalist and bourgeois values. Less than a year after seizing power Lenin ordered his People's Commissar for Justice to search the state archives and destroy 'all deeds of landholdings, factories and real property and so on and so forth . . . secretly and with no publicity'.[1] Inheritance was abolished and since middle-class power was rooted in property ownership, the intention was clearly to dash the hopes of a bourgeois restoration.

PEACE

For the Bolsheviks the Russian revolution was merely the first phase of the revolution that would, according to their Marxist beliefs, engulf the whole world. Certainly, in late 1917, after three years of carnage and waste of life – workers' lives, Lenin would argue – it seemed reasonable to many that only the overthrow of the warring regimes would end the suffering. Indeed, in the weeks following the October coup, the Bolsheviks were encouraged by unrest and mutinies in neighbouring countries and armies to think that a more general revolution was imminent.

Lenin's first concern, however, was not world revolution but the consolidation of his own regime. He had promised peace and had gained the support, or at least the acquiescence, of the army, which had enabled him to seize power, and now he must deliver if his regime was to survive. He must withdraw Russia from the war, whatever the cost. As he expected, his call to the Western powers to enter peace talks was peremptorily dismissed, thus freeing him to deal with the Germans. In any case, he had a debt to repay to them.

The Bolsheviks held sway in the capitals and most of central Russia, and were steadily gaining power in the eastern provinces. But the Don Cossacks had established an anti-Bolshevik independent government in southern Russia, the Ukrainians had done the same in Kiev, and the Poles, Finns and Baltic peoples were striving for the same ends. The German army, moreover, was poised to strike at Petrograd itself.

An armistice was duly signed in the western Russian city of Brest-Litovsk in mid-December 1917 and peace talks began. The Germans, feeling themselves masters of the situation, began dictating terms. But it was not in the nature of Trotsky, the Soviet foreign commissar who had not a single day's experience of diplomacy, to bow the knee to anyone, least of all to German militarists. The Bolsheviks were also well aware of the parlous state of the German military economy and knew that the Germans needed peace on the Eastern Front no less than they did themselves. There was no need to kowtow.

At Brest-Litovsk Trotsky conducted a dual policy: he rattled the stiff-backed German delegates with fiery revolutionary rhetoric and dismissed their peace terms, but also declared that the Russian army would not go on fighting. It was a policy, he said, of 'neither war nor peace'. The puzzled Germans took this to mean that the armistice was terminated and in February 1918 they advanced their troops deeper into Russia. Lenin sued for peace but was answered with even tougher demands: Soviet Russia must hand over all of her non-Russian territories in the west, Poland, Finland and the Baltic states, and recognize the independence of Ukraine, where in fact the Germans and Austrians were already in occupation and intended to remain.

The Bolshevik government was split. Lenin was for accepting Germany's terms: Germany was on its last legs, he argued; the treaty wouldn't matter. The opposition felt that peace on these terms would postpone European revolution by allowing Germany to face the Allies in the West with greater force. Lenin won the argument by threatening to resign and the treaty was signed on 14 March 1918. In November 1917, in order to widen the base of his political support, Lenin had given a small number of government posts to Left Socialist Revolutionaries. This party had split off from the large Party of Socialist Revolutionaries that had kept alive the spirit of nineteenth-century Populism, in particular the interests of Russia's vast peasant population. The Brest-Litovsk agreement was too much for them to take and they left the government in protest. The Treaty of Brest-Litovsk was ratified the next day.

Russia was compelled to give up one quarter of her most developed area, three quarters of her iron and steel industry, three quarters of her coal mines, a quarter of her cultivated area, a quarter of her railways, a third of her textile industry and fifty-six million of her population. And the treaty did nothing to remove German forces from large areas of southern Russia. Also, under the treaty, Lenin gave Germany 245.5 tons of gold and later, in the autumn of 1918 when Germany was facing imminent defeat, Lenin handed over a further 95 tons of gold.

DEFENDING THE REVOLUTION

Lenin's first priority was to hold on to power. He had no guarantee that his regime enjoyed the support of a majority of the population and he had thought it wise to offer a few places in his government to Left Socialist Revolutionaries. Not until 1989, when Mikhail Gorbachev instituted the Congress of People's Deputies, did such democratic elections take place in Russia as those for the Constituent Assembly, and when it finally convened, in January 1918, it emerged that the Bolsheviks had won only 168 out of the total number of 703 seats, while the Socialist Revolutionaries and their allies, the Ukrainian SRs and other ethnic minority SRs, had gained 399. All the other parties, including the Mensheviks and Kadets, had done very badly indeed, reflecting the mood of impatience that had overcome the Russian electorate after eight months of vacillation by the Provisional Government.

Lenin's solution to this new and unexpected situation was to declare that the October revolution had rendered the Constituent Assembly redundant, and to prevent the deputies from meeting on the second day by the use of armed force. Russia's most democratically elected assembly had met for only one day. 'Everything has turned out for the best,' Lenin said. 'The dissolution of the Assembly means the complete and open repudiation of democracy in favour of dictatorship. This will be a valuable lesson.' The public, exhausted by war, strikes, revolution and general mayhem, did not react to this trampling of their short-lived democracy, though many shared the belief that they were indeed learning a lesson.

Clearly the Bolsheviks had many enemies who wanted them destroyed. Only six weeks after seizing power, in December 1917, Lenin created the Cheka, or the Extraordinary Commission for Combating Counter-revolution and Sabotage. As the Bolsheviks' eyes and ears, as well as its chief enforcer, the Cheka was the first of a long series of agencies which gave the Soviet Union its particular character as a police state. At first, 'counter-revolutionaries' virtually identified themselves as open enemies of Communism and indeed were the core of the White movement, which came into being in the spring of 1918 with the aim of mobilizing Russia against the Reds. To deal with this major threat to its existence the regime had to form its own army – the Worker Peasant Red Army – and fight a bitter if ultimately successful civil war.

A majority of the educated and propertied population would seek to find a *modus vivendi* with the new regime but a substantial minority, numbering some two million people, would find an escape route out of the country, either by fortuitous emigration or deportation. Those who remained behind were soon disabused of the idea that the regime wanted to find a *modus vivendi* with them. By exclusion from work, which alone entitled a citizen to a food ration, by constant harassment and persecution, by exile and imprisonment, and ultimately by physical destruction, Lenin showed that his declared aim had been no idle threat. By 1921 the process would be complete and would include the Mensheviks. As for the working classes in whose name the revolution had been made, their trade unions were quickly brought under Communist control as the regime began to wrestle with the country's economic problems and would brook neither criticism nor opposition.

WAR COMMUNISM

Bolshevik economic policy emerged from the contingencies of the time. Beyond vague and utopian notions in an undefined sort of socialist planning for the good of society, Marxism had provided little guidance for 'building socialism'. Lenin himself had declared in 1917 that the workers themselves – guided by 'their' party, the Communists – would organize industrial production. Having excluded the old property owners from the economy, the proletarian revolution would achieve its goal by utilizing the achievements of capitalism. 'Capitalism,' he wrote in 1917 in *State and Revolution*, 'has created an accounting *apparatus* in the shape of the banks, syndicates, postal service, consumers' societies, and office employees' unions. *Without big banks socialism would be impossible*. The big banks *are* the state apparatus.'[2] Of course by nationalizing them after October Lenin ensured that they could not function as banks in any meaningful sense, and thus he hobbled his own efforts at economic recovery at the outset, even if only in his own terms.

Once in power Lenin resorted almost exclusively to harsh draconian measures to solve virtually any problem. The peasants, to whom he had promised land, soon found that the forcible collection of grain and other agricultural produce by armed Bolshevik gangs reduced them once more to little more than state vassals. All private trade was banned, most of industry was nationalized, central control was imposed on the production and distribution of goods, and the almost worthless currency was replaced by a system of barter. In practice the system, which was given the politically correct name of 'War Communism', was little more than organized chaos. So fragmented was the country itself at this time that the economy could not realistically be managed on a national scale, but functioned instead on a haphazard local basis. Private trade was replaced by a rampant black market, where only some foreign currencies had any monetary worth.

By the spring and early summer of 1918 euphoria at the October victory had become disillusionment. The large cities were starving and it was already clear that slogans and decrees were not solving the country's huge problems.

REDS AND WHITES

Armed resistance to the new regime arose almost at once, when tsarist General Alexeyev set up his

Volunteer Army in the Don Cossack region at the end of 1917. In March 1918 Lenin moved the seat of government to Moscow, where he felt safer, and by the summer of 1918 the Bolsheviks were facing significant armed opposition, much of it stirred up by anger at the Treaty of Brest-Litovsk.

Nicholas II and his family had been arrested by the Provisional Government in March 1917 and after five months were moved to Tobolsk in Western Siberia. In April 1918 they were taken into custody by the local Bolsheviks and taken to Yekaterinburg in the Urals, where they were held in the mansion of a former rich merchant which was dubbed the 'House of Special Purpose'. Lenin had intended to put Nicholas on trial but in the summer of 1918, with the Cossacks having risen and the old tsarist officer corps organizing themselves, he feared that Nicholas might serve as a live banner to rally the Whites. Thus it was that on 17 July 1918 the local Bolsheviks of Yekaterinburg murdered the entire royal family, acting on the orders of the Politburo in Moscow.

Resistance to the regime was further stimulated by the savagery of Bolshevik policy. An attempt was made on Lenin's life at the end of August 1918 and served to unleash a wave of reprisals which was given the official name of the Red Terror. Summary executions became commonplace. 'Class enemies' were put into concentration camps, priests were killed, hostages were taken in the countryside to enforce grain collection and at times Lenin had to upbraid his own comrades for behaving like 'milksops' when they found his harsh orders unpalatable.

White militancy was now redoubled by a sense that Russia had been taken over by an evil force and that their cause was the very salvation of the country, rather than the restoration of any particular political regime.

The opposition – which went under the general catch-all name of the White Movement – proliferated around almost the entire periphery of the new Soviet Republic, from the Arctic to the south and on to Siberia and the Far East. Because the ethnic and political mixture was at its richest in Ukraine, the war was at its most complex there.

Aided at various times by Allied Interventionist forces, which sought at first to bring Russia back into the war, and then after the German surrender in November 1918 to restore a regime that was friendly to the West, the White armies were from the outset crippled by a lack of unified leadership. They scored a number of impressive local victories over the Communists on several occasions, and in the spring of 1919 it appeared they might even capture Moscow and finish the Bolsheviks off. The Secretary of the Politburo, Yakov Sverdlov, had several false passports and a large amount of currency in his safe, ready, it may be assumed, for Lenin and his closest entourage to use if the worst happened.

But the Bolsheviks were assisted by a number of advantages which the Whites lacked. First, in strategic terms, it was relatively easier to fight from within a circle which was centred on the Russian heartland, while their enemies were strung out along an almost endless perimeter. Second, the Bolsheviks could rally the workers and peasants with slogans which persuaded them that they were fighting both for their own state and also against the restoration of a landowners' and capitalists' state. Third, the Whites lacked a common purpose, divided as they were between monarchists and republicans, liberals and reactionaries, national liberationists who sympathized with the aspirations of the minorities fighting at their sides, and Russian chauvinists who wanted nothing but the old borders of the Empire to be retrieved. And finally the Whites had no charismatic leader with the intelligence and organizing ability of Leon Trotsky who built the Red Army, mobilized former tsarist officers and created political commisars to shadow them, and sustained its morale throughout the civil war, often by the use of the harshest discipline.

Both sides employed savage methods to mobilize and retain support. The Bolsheviks reintroduced the death penalty for desertion and used it as a deterrent to anyone who tried to evade military service. The peasants, broadly speaking, were indifferent to both Red and White propaganda, although they may have been slightly more inclined to fight alongside Reds than Whites, whom they identified with the old land-owning class.

In the spring of 1919 a threat from a completely different quarter arose. The government of independent Poland decided to retrieve its former lands in Russia. Knowing that the White military were dominated by Russian nationalists who would not assist the Poles in their territorial claims on Russia, the Poles did not attempt to form an alliance, but rather calculated that the new Soviet state was weak and vulnerable. Lenin was in no mood to take on yet another foe and adopted a peaceful approach. Poland was in a desperate condition, with millions sick and receiving famine relief from the American Relief Administration under Herbert Hoover, yet it set out on this aggressive path.

In April 1919 the Polish army captured the ancient Polish-Lithuanian city of Vilna (Wilno in Polish, Vilnius in Lithuania today), followed by Minsk in the following August. In April 1920 the Poles invaded Ukraine with spectacular success but by June the Red Army had driven them back out of Russia, and stood on the Polish border. The question was discussed in the Politburo of what to do now. Should the Red Army press ahead in the expectation that the Polish people would rise against their bourgeois government and join the Reds in a revolutionary war, taking the revolution into Europe?

Trotsky and others opposed such an adventure, knowing as they did that the Poles were neither ripe for socialist revolution nor likely to support the forces of a country that had held Poland in chains for two hundred years. But Lenin was adamant. As one of his biographers put it, 'He believed in the export of revolution on the tip of the bayonet . . . and he would teach Poland a lesson by setting her aflame'.[3]

Lenin's Communist 'crusade' against the government of Poland quickly came to grief. The Polish workers rallied to the defence of their newly independent country and in August the Red Army was defeated at the gates of Warsaw. By October 1920 Lenin was compelled to accept an armistice and in 1921 he signed the Treaty of Riga which gave Poland large White Russian (Belorussian) and Ukrainian territory which the Soviet Union would not retrieve until 1939. Lenin now agreed with Trotsky's argument that Soviet intervention had hindered the development of socialist revolution in Poland and that the invasion had been a mistake. Future Soviet leaders would not be so ready to admit an error of such magnitude.

By the end of 1920 the remnants of the White armies had been driven into the Crimea, where they joined and were joined by tens of thousands of ordinary citizens seeking an escape from the violence, dispossession, disease and general chaos that was Russia. The British and French navies, which were part of the Intervention, helped to evacuate these unfortunates to Constantinople. The Bolsheviks had won the civil war.

SIX

The New Regime

The civil war had been as savage as anything experienced in Russia's bloodstained history. Both sides used terror, hostage-taking, summary execution. But the ideology, and no less the state purpose which motivated the Bolsheviks, aimed to create not merely a state that was entirely under their control but a society as well. The Whites had nothing in their minds approaching these aims.

Throughout his adult life Lenin had shown himself to be a 'control freak', in today's slang. He had manipulated Party committees and other agencies to conform to his ideas, and cast aside close comrades who disagreed with him, regardless of the fact that the number of his supporters in the dog years after 1905 were dwindling rapidly, chiefly because of his dictatorial and unreasonable manner. He had conceived of the Party as an orchestra, where only one conductor could operate successfully, a conductor who knew each player's strengths and weaknesses. Or as an army, which could only function properly under a single general.

He thought of the organization of the state in the same way, as an organism which worked like a well-oiled machine, controlled by a single – and single-minded – operator. And society, which must be made to function classlessly and harmoniously, would similarly only do so if a single intelligence, i.e. Lenin and his like-minded Party, were in full control.

Lenin closed down the non-Bolshevik press; through the Cheka he hounded then banned other political parties, imprisoning, exiling or deporting their members; he used public hangings, not merely as punishment, but as examples to the rest of the local population; he emasculated the trade unions and enforced labour discipline by exploiting the food shortages: those who worked, ate. But the food rations were not equal for all workers: some categories who were favoured by the regime got more than their fellow workers, and this aroused resentment. Workers left their factories to forage in the surrounding villages, to buy or barter food from the peasants. The Bolsheviks banned this form of self-help, which they labelled black-marketing or speculation, and set up roadblocks to search men returning to town, confiscating the produce and prosecuting the culprits.

The Communist Party hierarchy was another matter. For them Lenin authorized a taste of the privileges that would come to characterize the whole system in due course: special rations, rest homes and good apartments, trips abroad for medical treatment, access to foreign currency and luxury goods, and so on. As for the Soviets, who in 1917 had ostensibly been handed power, by manipulation, intimidation and sheer physical force, the Communists rapidly brought them under their control.

THE PEASANTS

The Imperial Russian Army had traditionally consisted overwhelmingly of peasants, with the officer corps staffed by members of the aristocracy and lesser nobility. Universal conscription, introduced in 1874, and the mobilization of 1914 and after brought the other classes into the army, including to a small extent the educated middle classes, making it a 'nation-in-arms', but in 1917 the lower ranks still consisted chiefly of peasants. The army was an army of 'peasants in uniform'.

It had been plain to Lenin that in order for his

seizure of power to succeed he must neutralize the Imperial Army, and this he did by spreading defeatist propaganda in the trenches in the summer of 1917. He had also encouraged the soldiers to fraternize with their German counterparts. This policy, although it accelerated the disintegration of the Russian Army, had little effect on the other side, where German officers, wearing privates' uniforms, took part in the charade, while keeping their propaganda-vulnerable troops well away from Bolshevik agitators. And when the Bolsheviks made their bid for power the army was nowhere to be seen, and when Lenin told the peasants they would inherit the land, he instigated the virtual demobilization of the army.

For their part the peasants had no interest in the revolution, beyond the fact that its leader seemed to have given them permission to seize the land. Once they had achieved this goal, they wanted to be left alone. When they discovered that the hand of the new regime was even heavier than that of the pre-revolutionary order and that they were not allowed to conduct their affairs as they wished, many young peasants left the village to join peasant resistance movements. There were also numerous instances of peasants who had fought in the Red Army going over to partisan detachments and fighting the Reds, once they felt the harsh severity of Soviet rule.

Before 1917 Trotsky had warned that the first enemy the Communists would have to fight was the Russian peasant. What he meant was that the peasant's interest was fundamentally opposed to Communism, in that the peasant wanted to work his land as an independent farmer and to succeed in this he required the existence of a market. Communism was opposed to the market, as such. How to find a *modus vivendi* with the peasant was thus one of Lenin's first priorities.

As we have seen, however, the regime inherited an urban economy in ruins and therefore, having nothing to sell the peasant in exchange for his produce, Lenin resorted to the forcible extraction of grain. But when armed squads came to take their stocks the peasants tried to hide them, sometimes even burning them, rather than hand them over to a hostile government. Many stopped growing for the market at all and produced only enough to feed themselves and their families.

The problems in the village were worsened by the fact that countless workers, finding it impossible to live on their poor wages in towns where they could find no food, returned to villages they might have left no more than ten years earlier. In a population so dominated by peasants, even workers who had lived for more than a generation in the town would have relatives in the countryside to go to. In the years of the civil war the population of the capital fell by as much as two-thirds.

NEW DISCONTENTS

During the civil war the government could, to some extent, justify the many hardships it imposed on the people by the need to 'defend the revolution'. Once the civil war was clearly over and the regime emerged victorious, such appeals lost their force. A sense of grievance and discontent soon developed as the population craved some respite from the suffering inflicted by seven years of war, revolution and civil war.

One source of discontent was the treatment meted out to Red Army men once the civil war was over. At the end of 1920 the regime decided to demobilize half a million men. The railways would not cope if they were all sent home at once. On the other hand, to keep them in the army would mean feeding and clothing them. In April 1921 Lenin ordered that the Red Army soldier should be given neither bread, nor clothes, nor boots. He must be given the choice of either leaving immediately and 'walk home with nothing', or 'wait a year on one-eighth of a pound of bread and no clothing or boots'. As Lenin cynically commented: 'He'll leave on his own and on foot.'[1]

Not all Red Army soldiers were permitted to go home, however. Many were kept back in the so-called Labour Army and were directed to work in whatever factories the government chose. Not only were these men naturally aggrieved but so also were the workers whose jobs they threatened by working – under duress – for virtually nothing.

Meanwhile the workers watched as Communists, who were given the best jobs and best wages, were being used as armed enforcers by the local Party bosses to ensure that ordinary workers carried out their orders.

By the winter of 1920 the pressure of discontent among the workers reached danger level. Hundreds of risings had taken place and in February 1921 strikes and demonstrations took place in all the major plants in Petrograd, calling for an end to the roadblocks and to the system of differential rations, and for Labour Army men to be withdrawn and Communist factory squads disarmed.

The Party leadership took a tough line. It imposed a curfew, banned street demonstrations and set up 'defence committees' in factories, backed by the Communist armed squads.

The spirit of 1917, however, was not dead in the Party. The Mensheviks had long ago accused Lenin of an exploitative and dictatorial attitude towards the workers. Now he was showing how right they had been and members of his own party were troubled by the same doubts. Many leading Bolsheviks were uneasy about leaning so heavily on the very people who had helped to bring them to power so recently. They felt that the harsh measures were a betrayal of the Party's ideology and its purpose. Various opposition groups came into being at this time.

One group, the Left Communists, may be described as fundamentalists: they opposed the Treaty of Brest-Litovsk, advocated the full implementation of socialist policies and rejected any compromise with capitalist interests, Russian or foreign. They attracted little support, as their views were seen as unrealistic and counter-productive.

In 1920 another group, called Democratic Centralists, expressed concern over the declining rights of Party members to express their opinions and to exert influence on the central institutions. They also wanted power restored to the Soviets.

A third group, the Workers Opposition, which

also emerged in 1920, was unhappy at the Party's treatment of the trade unions which, they felt, should be running industry. It was an appeal they made to the Lenin of 1917 who had said at a time when he was striving to overthrow the old Russia, that within twenty-four hours after the overthrow of capitalism, simple workers would be able to control production; there would be no need for material incentives, all officials, managers and similar personnel would be paid a worker's wage. By 1921, however, Lenin had undergone a radical change of mind. He had seen the chaos caused when the workers were in control under War Communism. Now he knew that it was a fantasy to suggest that ordinary workers were capable of administering the state. They would take years to learn.

Lenin conducted a successful campaign against opposition tendencies in the Party with the help of Trotsky, who spelled out what Lenin was thinking with brutal frankness. It was sheer nonsense, Trotsky said, to talk about proletarian democracy when Russia's economy was in ruins and required military methods to get going again. The unions and the workers had to be strictly controlled by the Party. All democratic and egalitarian compunction had to yield to the drive for higher production. Marxism, he reminded the Party, as Stalin was to do in future years, never promised equality until the final stage of abundance under full communism was reached. Men work because they have to and work well because of material incentives.

And the Party was run on Leninist principles, which dictated that policy, the programme and all other business should be determined by the centre, i.e. the Politburo. This meant that all these opposition groups were necessarily opposing a 'Party line' and to do so invariably provoked the cry from the centre that they were threatening to split the Party, which was as serious a political crime as any. And because the majority of the members would inevitably support the centre which gave them their position, their living, their privileges and their security, the centre always won.

This relationship between the Party and its members, important as it was in Lenin's day, would acquire a literally murderous quality under his successor, Joseph Stalin. While none of these groups represented a real threat to the leadership, they nevertheless pricked the Party's proletarian conscience and were an irritant that Lenin felt it important to eradicate.

A particularly militant centre of support for the

Soviets in 1917 and after was the island garrison of Kronstadt. Located about twenty miles from Petrograd in the Gulf of Finland, and only five miles from the mainland town of Oranienbaum, the soldiers and sailors of Kronstadt had played a significant role in the seizure of power, as well as in the civil war. They were regarded as true champions of the new Soviet order. By the spring of 1921, however, they were thoroughly disillusioned with the Bolshevik regime. They wanted an immediate return to what they perceived as the true revolutionary path of 1917, with the Soviets holding power, and an end to the abuses and arrogance of the new Party bureaucrats and commissars.

On 1 March 1921 a mass meeting in the centre of Kronstadt endorsed a fifteen-point resolution that reflected the mood of the strikers of Petrograd. It amounted to nothing less than a demand for the peaceful dismantling of the Communist police state, the abolition of War Communism and the internal reform of the Soviet system. Privileged rations, roadblocks and armed Communist factory squads must be abolished, the workers must be 'disenserfed' and permitted to move from one job to another, peasants must be free to use the land as they wished and craftsmen allowed to practice, although neither group should use hired labour. There must be freedom of speech and assembly, freedom of workers' and peasants' unions, non-Communists must be allowed to start their own newspapers and issue propaganda, and there must be secret elections to new Soviets with left-wing socialists and anarchists allowed to take part.

The resolution emphatically did *not* call for the restoration of the monarchy or the old landlords, nor for the desired civil and political freedoms to be extended to the bourgeoisie. It was in effect a socialist charter and purely revolutionary in its intent. And as such it was entirely unacceptable to the Leninist leadership of the government, which set up a tight blockade of the island and refused adamantly to negotiate. Trotsky declared that either the rebels surrender unconditionally, or 'you will be shot like partridges'.[2] The government condemned the rebels as Whites and counter-revolutionaries and Soviet historiography did not correct this picture until the 1980s.

The Kronstadt rebels had not expected that they would have to fight the government. They had imagined that their appeal would find an echo throughout the working classes of Russia and bring the government to its senses. Had they been more strategically minded they would have waited two or three weeks before coming out in open rebellion, for the ice would have melted and made an invasion of the island virtually impossible. The thaw would also have freed two ice-bound battleships that could have been manoeuvred and used for defence.

Instead, for two weeks they fought bitter battles and held off the Red Army units sent to subdue them. Finally the government 'got tough' and on 17 March some 45–50,000 Red Army troops were sent across the ice to crush the insurgency, and by the next day they had accomplished their aim. About 15,000 soldiers and sailors were killed in battle and only recently have the archives revealed that 2,329 soldiers and sailors were executed, and 6,459 were imprisoned or exiled, only to be shot later by Stalin. The archives have also revealed that Lenin's commander, Tukhachevsky, intended using poison gas against the insurgents and was only prevented from doing so by the late arrival of the barrels.

NEP

By the winter of 1920, with the civil war virtually over, it was clear that the hoped-for revolution in Western Europe was not going to happen in the foreseeable future. The changes that had taken place were certainly momentous: the Austro-Hungarian and German Empires had collapsed and several successor states came into being; Poland was independent; a civil war in Finland had culminated in the victory of a White regime; and some of the territory ceded by Lenin to Germany in 1918 remained in non-Russian hands after the defeat of Germany and the repudiation of the Treaty of Brest-Litovsk.

But the idea that the Russian revolution would ignite world revolution was not now on the immediate agenda. (This did not prevent Lenin from authorizing the transfer of vast sums of money to Communist parties elsewhere in the world for the purpose of organizing revolution, a practice that would continue throughout the Communist era.) Lenin had told the party that a socialist revolution could only prevail in a peasant country on two conditions: it must be supported in good time by a socialist revolution in an advanced country and there must be an agreement between the proletariat – by which he meant the Communist Party – and the majority peasant population. With the failure of the first, the second became all the more important. With so many domestic preoccupations Lenin now began to speak of 'socialism in one country', a slogan usually attributed to Stalin.

The Kronstadt revolt brought home to Lenin the extent of dissatisfaction with his regime. His solution has commonly been described as evidence of his greatness as a statesman, though it would be more accurate to see it as evidence of his genius as a politician.

Food shortage had played a key part in bringing down the tsarist regime and now Lenin understood the fundamental importance of being able to feed the workers. The rouble was worth a tenth of its pre-war value, while bread had gone up in cost more than eleven times. The workers were stealing virtually any moveable object in their factories to barter for food, including the leather transmission belts on their machines to sell for repairing boots. Land under cultivation fell by more than one third. Horses and livestock also fell dramatically – as did wages – while the cost of living rose to five times that of 1916.

The only source of food in Russia was the peasant farmer. Force had been tried and had failed. It was therefore vital to devise a system that would induce the peasants to grow more produce and to sell it to the state or in a real market. Sooner or later the system of War Communism would undoubtedly have been given up as unworkable but to find an alternative that would appear politically acceptable was a daunting task.

In effect Lenin surrendered to the peasants. He told the Tenth Congress: 'We know that only by agreement with them can we save the socialist revolution in Russia, as long as it has not advanced in other countries. We are sufficiently sober politicians to be able to speak our minds. Let us reconsider our policy.' Since threats as well as promises had failed, he now advocated freedom of trade for the small producer and the production of consumer goods in the towns to be exchanged for agricultural produce. There was much opposition from the left wing of the party but Lenin had his way. The main feature of his New Economic Policy (NEP) was a tax in kind, designed to assure the peasants that everything above a strictly defined amount was theirs to dispose of as they chose.

Above all the peasants were to be made safe from arbitrary requisitions of grain and forced sales at fixed prices. Instead they were encouraged to develop a surplus for sale at a profit. As the former Left Communist Nikolai Bukharin told them: 'Get rich!'

PARTY UNITY

Lenin realized that freedom of trade would lead to a
revival of capitalism in the country but he rightly saw
that personal incentive through trade was the only
possible way to revive the dying embers of the
economy. Trade was anathema to the Marxists but it
would give the peasants the incentive to produce
more and thus stimulate an improvement in
agriculture in general. Once that had been achieved
the state-owned industries would be restored and all
private enterprise displaced. When strength and
resources had been accumulated, a powerful
industry could be created as the economic founda-
tion of socialism. Then, and only then, could a
determined offensive be undertaken to destroy the
remnants of capitalism in the whole country,
including the countryside. How long it would take to
reach this goal was not made clear. Sometimes it
seemed NEP was to be a short-term expedient. At
other times, Lenin talked of it as a serious under-
taking that would last a long time. In all probability
he had no clear idea himself.

NEP was thus rationalized as a temporary retreat,
a respite that would enable the Party to leap forward
more audaciously when the time was ripe. And the

new policy achieved quite quickly what it had aimed for, particularly in small trade and artisan industry. The peasants in the central provinces began to function again and the state began rebuilding the industrial economy. By 1927 industrial output was back to a level roughly comparable to or better than it had been in 1913, which was a peak year.

The defeat of the Whites, the Kronstadt revolt and the adoption of NEP, however, did not mean the end of internal strife. Throughout 1921 and 1922 peasant rebellions flared up in thirty-six provinces, where the ruined economy was showing no signs of recovery. In 1921 alone the Red Army lost 171,185 men in internal disorders. Famine was breaking out and the towns were underfed.

With millions starving, Lenin was forced – after some ungrateful haggling – to permit the American Relief Administration to extend its field operations to Russia, making sure that the mostly young relief workers were watched closely by the security organs. The conditions were horrific, with cannibalism a widespread phenomenon. In the summer of 1922 Maxim Gorky, who had issued a worldwide appeal for help, felt able to write to Herbert Hoover, the chief of the relief administration: ' . . . in the history of practical humanitarianism I know of no accomplishment which in terms of magnitude and generosity can be compared to the relief that you have actually accomplished.'[3]

The relief programme was abruptly terminated in June 1923 when it emerged that the government was selling large quantities of grain abroad to raise foreign currency, instead of feeding the people. What did not emerge was that it was also sending vast quantities of tsarist gold reserves and confiscated church treasures out of the country to support foreign Communist parties.

PARTY POLITICS

On the political front the party began to prepare for the next offensive. The line adopted by Lenin, and promulgated by Bukharin – who acquired a reputation as the 'high priest' of NEP – was that the Party should make all the economic concessions it possibly could but make no political concessions at all. To those who imagined that economic freedom would lead to political freedom Bukharin gave the blunt answer that economic concessions were being made in order to ensure that the Party was not forced to make political concessions.

Lenin knew that free elections would sweep the

Communists out of power. And since it was a basic tenet of his ideology that only the Communists were capable of bringing socialism to Russia, free elections were out of the question. To maintain this position in the face of so much dissension and discontent the Party must not be allowed to split, it must remain united, observing Bolshevik discipline in the way he had described twenty years earlier, in his book *What is to be Done?* (1902), but had never achieved in practice. His was a simple formula: the country would be under total Communist control and the Communist Party would be under the total control of the leadership, which meant him.

The Kronstadt revolt took place while the Tenth Congress of the Party was in progress. Indeed, 300 of the delegates promptly left Moscow to join, or lead, the Red Army in its final murderous assault on the rebels.

When Bukharin spoke of denying political concessions, he had in mind not only the peasants, the bourgeoisie and other socialist parties: no concessions were to be made to the various oppositions within the Communist Party itself, either. The Tenth Congress was confronted with the demand by Lenin and his supporters in the Politburo that henceforth no Party member should be allowed to form a separate faction on the basis of a difference with the centre.

The principle that the centre was always right prevailed and the Congress ordered all factional groups within the Party dissolved and prohibited them from farming or presenting a common platform in the future. In a secret resolution the Central Committee was given the power to expel Party members – including members of the Central Committee itself – for engaging in what came to be called factionalism.

Lenin and Trotsky won their battle but at the price of giving up what remained of democracy inside the Party. They thereby helped to prepare the way for its further erosion and the victory of the Party bureaucracy and the Party's chief bureaucrat, Stalin.

SEVEN

The Cultural Revolution

It was a basic tenet of all radical Russian thought, dating back to the middle of the nineteenth century, that the elimination of illiteracy and cultural backwardness were two essential prerequisites for the success of a social revolution. Lenin and the Bolsheviks, however, had not given much thought to the question of how their government, once in power, would deal with these issues. In cultural terms Lenin was a conservative, rather prudish and somewhat condescending to the Modernist movement that swept through European art and culture at the beginning of the century. As far as education was concerned – his wife, Nadezhda Krupskaya, was a former schoolteacher and took a special interest – he was of the opinion that as long as the schools worked it was enough for the time being. And soon many more Russians were being taught to read and write as thousands of new schools were opened, and although they were mostly primitive and lacking in proper buildings and school books, they functioned.

REVOLUTION AND THE ARTS

The People's Commissar for Public Enlightenment, Anatoly Lunacharsky, himself a playwright of no great distinction, was very much committed to involving the world of learning and the arts in the cause of the revolution. He struggled with the leadership for funds to improve the condition of schools and education in general, and he encouraged other playwrights and actors to feel themselves part of the great new adventure. Indeed the first anniversary of the October revolution was commemorated in Petrograd with a re-enactment of the storming of the Winter Palace. Hosts of artists and actors were recruited, along with thousands of extras, and so enthusiastic was the whole ensemble that more people were killed by accident than had been in the event itself.

In sweeping away the tsarist autocracy and its heavy handed bureaucracy, the February revolution cleared the ground for a society without discrimination, whether it be of a class, political, ethnic, religious or economic kind. In the minds of many the October revolution took the liberation process further and faster. Many artists, certainly those Russian artists who dominated the European avant-garde, saw 1917 as the end of the era of bourgeois hypocrisy, cultural backwardness and old-fashioned ways of living and working, and thought it heralded the dawn of a new age: a machine age of planned organization, of science, technology and fundamental principles, of self-awareness. As revolutionaries in art, they felt a natural affinity with the social revolution promised by the Bolsheviks.

But Lunarcharsky's inclinations soon led him to mobilize not only the artists who sympathized with the revolution but also those who represented the cultural institutions of the pre-revolutionary era, putting them to work organizing education and culture for the new society. The first question to be addressed was the definition of the art of the proletariat which, at least in name, now ruled. For Lunacharsky the issue was practical rather than ideological, improvised rather than planned. He simply looked for capable individuals and put them in charge of the new institutions – museums, theatres, literary journals, schools and universities. Equally, although he gave the impression of being a partisan of the avant-garde, he believed that the culture of the past must be put to the service of the new Soviet society and that if proletarian culture was to rise above that of the past, it must build on the cultural heritage, Russian and foreign, and not destroy it.

The avant-garde argued that the new society must have a new art; just as its technology would be the most advanced, so its art must be modern and experimental, i.e. the art they practised. Revolutionary policies, they reasoned, must apply to culture as to politics. The Modernists had always assumed that there was a natural affinity between their own revolutionary purpose and that of the Bolsheviks, and had justifiably thought that their friend, Lunacharsky, would take their side against the artists of the old order, especially the academic practitioners in painting and the naturalists in the theatre. But their insistence that artists, not politicians, should design the future life of mankind made them unmanageable. This was not surprising, since they were instinctively and ideologically independently minded people who had always resisted interference from outside.

By 1922 Lunacharsky, the realist, was giving the bulk of his limited budget to conservative groups in the arts who would produce images that were accessible to the masses. He closed the revolutionary Free Artists' studio and helped to form the Association of Artists of Revolutionary Russia, a body that was fiercely opposed to everything the avant-garde stood for, and whose slogan was 'heroic realism'. Here were the successors of the Social Realists of the nineteenth century and the forerunners of the Union of Soviet Artists, formed ten years later, whose guiding principle was Socialist Realism.

Some avant-garde artists, who were content to remain in Soviet Russia and work with the regime, found a satisfactory compromise by getting involved in graphics and photography and indeed were responsible for putting these forms of Soviet art on the highest level of achievement by world standards.

Writers were in the most sensitive area of the creative arts. The first serious criticism of the tsarist regime had come from writers in the nineteenth century and Russian literature was noted for its concern with social issues. How would writers regard the new regime? What social issues would they alight on as the acid test of Communist intentions? The regime's promise of renewal appealed to many but its hatred and persecution of particular social classes aroused anxiety. Maxim Gorky, who was one of

Russia's best known writers, had supported Lenin before the revolution, both morally and financially, but as soon as the Bolsheviks began closing down the presses of other parties and taking over the Soviets by manipulation, Gorky castigated them harshly.

Gorky was a good example of the differences that would inevitably arise between the new regime, determined as it was to convey a clear message of socialist purpose to the people, and writers who saw the revolution as a liberating force that would unleash all of society's creative energy. As it became clear by 1921 to 1922 that the Party was taking over the creative institutions and promoting those who would make their career by doing its bidding, an exodus of writers and artists took place, many of them returning to their old pre-revolutionary haunts in Paris and Berlin, where they would flourish or expire, cut off from the experience of their native land.

Postscript

Ironically it was the unbridling of writers that led to the demise of the Soviet Union. First, under Khrushchev, for about a decade from the mid-1950s, the Party sought to re-energize society by allowing writers to express themselves in ways other than those prescribed by the Party, and even to explore themes that had been frowned on, to say the least. The exercise was strictly controlled and severely limited in scope but it still unleashed a spirit of criticism and objectivity that led eventually to the mentality of the 1980s, when Mikhail Gorbachev, as General Secretary of the Party, launched his policy of *glasnost*, or openness.

At first it was writers and playwrights who tested the water, using the Stalin years as the safest area to explore, since it had already been partly exposed by Khrushchev in 1956 and then resealed by Brezhnev. Then journalists began writing in detail about the parlous state the country had got into. They found that the economy and the environment were in ruins, the political system corrupt from top to bottom, the country's history told as nothing but a tissue of lies. Soon they were joined by the traditionally more cautious historians and, as they dug deeper, they found layer after layer of falsehood and eventually came to the revolution of 1917 itself.

Apart from unreconstructed Communists in Russia today there are very few people who regard the October revolution as the dawn of a new age.

Notes

CHAPTER TWO

1. Hynes, A.L. and Vulliamy, C.E. (eds), *The Letters of the Tsar to the Tsaritsa, 1914–1917*, London, The Bodley Head, 1929, p. 77.
2. Ibid., p. 150.
3. Cited in Shukman, H., *Lenin and the Russian Revolution*, London, Batsford, 1966, p. 151.

CHAPTER THREE

1. Avdeev, N., *Revolyutsiya 1917 goda*, vol. 1, Moscow, 1923, pp. 13–14.
2. Cited in Shukman, H. *Lenin and the Russian Revolution*, London, Batsford, 1966, p. 171.

CHAPTER FOUR

1. Reed, John. *Ten Days that Shook the World*, new illustrated edition, Stroud, Gloucestershire, Sutton Publishing, 1997, p. 78.

CHAPTER FIVE

1. Volkogonov, Dmitri. *The Rise and Fall of the Soviet Empire*, translated and edited by Harold Shukman, London, HarperCollins, 1998, p. 76.
2. Kowalski, Ronald. *The Russian Revolution 1917–1921*, London, Routledge, 1997, p. 84.
3. Fischer, Louis. *The Life of Lenin*, London, Weidenfeld and Nicolson, 1964, p. 393.

CHAPTER SIX

1. Volkogonov, Dmitri. *The Rise and Fall of the Soviet Empire*, translated and edited by Harold Shukman, London, HarperCollins, 1998, p. 77.
2. Getzler, I. 'The Kronstadt Revolt', in Harold Shukman (ed.) *The Blackwell Encyclopedia of the Russian Revolution*, Oxford, Blackwell, 1988, p. 159.
3. Cited in Figes, Orlando. *A People's Tragedy: The Russian Revolution, 1891–1924*, London, Pimlico, 1996, p. 780.

Further Reading

Figes, Orlando. *A People's Tragedy: The Russian Revolution, 1891–1924* (London, Pimlico, 1996). This is a highly readable book in which the author successfully interweaves the history of the revolution with the lives of ordinary people, and highlights the relations between the centre and the regions.

Pipes, Richard. *The Russian Revolution, 1899–1917* (London, Collins Harvill, 1990), and *Russia Under the Bolshevik Regime, 1919–1924* (London, Collins Harvill, 1994). These two works together represent a closely detailed analysis of the events based on a particularly wide and original range of sources.

Reed, John. *Ten Days that Shook the World* (illustrated edition, Stroud, Gloucestershire, Sutton Publishing Ltd, 1997). An eyewitness account of October 1917 by an American journalist, this book was endorsed by Lenin. It contains perceptive observations of leading figures.

Rogger, Hans. *Russia in the Age of Modernisation and Revolution, 1881–1917* (London, Longman, 1983). A standard work providing descriptive and analytical accounts of all classes of society against a background of industrial development and political upheaval.

Shukman, Harold (ed). *The Blackwell Encyclopedia of the Russian*

Revolution (Oxford, Blackwell, 1994). Articles by an international panel of distinguished specialists on all aspects of the revolution, with biographical entries on a wide range of personalities.

Trotsky, Leon. *My Life* (New York, The Universal Library, 1960). One of the most vivid accounts of the events by one of its most important participants.

Volkogonov, Dmitri. *Lenin: Life and Legacy*, translated and edited by Harold Shukman (London, HarperCollins, 1995). Based on Lenin's unpublished archives, the first work published in Russia that attacks Lenin as Stalin's predecessor.

Index

Bold type indicates main or more significant entries.

Alexander II, Tsar 5, 11–12
Alexander III, Tsar 12
Alexandra (Alix), Empress 18–19, 22, 25–6, **26–7**, 32, 71
Alexei, Tsarevich 18–21, 37–8
Alexeyev, General Mikhail 70–1
Allied Interventionist forces 72, 76
army *see* Imperial Russian Army; Red Army
Armenians 43
art **100–3**
Aurora (cruiser) 59
Austro-Hungarian Empire 90

Baltic states 64–5
Black Hundreds 16–17
Bloody Sunday (1905) 13
Bolsheviks; ideology vii, 43, 77, 84
  before Revolution 2–5, 41–2, 46–50, 53
  Revolution **56–60**
  after Revolution 61–3, 67–8, **70–6**, 78–9
  'War Communism' **69–70**, 85, 91–2

see also Communist Party
Brezhnev, Leonid 105
Brusilov, General Alexei 29
Bukharin, Nikolai 44, 92, 95–7

capitalism 10, 69, 93
Central War Industries Committee 28–9, 32–3
Cheka 67–8, 78–9
Civil War **66–76**, 77
class war 10, 49, 62
Communist Party 61, 79, 90, **95–7**, 106
  see also Bolsheviks
Congress of People's Deputies 66
Constituent Assembly 46, 58–9, 66–7
Copenhagen 47–8
Cossacks 35, 63, 70–1
Crimea 76
Cultural Revolution **99–104**

death penalty 17, 55, 74, 78
democracy; elections to Duma 13–14, 15–16

elections to Constituent Assembly
58–9, 66–7
suppression of 87–8, 95–7
Democratic Centralist group 84
Dmitri Pavlovich, Grand Duke 31–2
Dual Power (Provisional
Government and Petrograd
Soviet) **45–50**
Duma 14, **15–18**, 24, 28, 30–3, 36–7,
39, 41

economy **69–70**, **89–92**, 93–4
education 12, 99–100

Finland 50, 56, 63, 64–5, 90
First World War; Russia enters **23–6**
and internal politics **27–33**, **40–50**,
52, 79–80
armistice **62–6**, 90
food and famine 35, 39, 68, 78, 91,
94–5
France 45–6, 76
Fundamental Laws 18

Georgia 41–2, 43
Germany *see* First World War
gold 66, 95
Gorbachev, Mikhail 66, 105
Goremykin, Prime Minister 29
Gorky, Maxim 94–5, 103–4
Great Britain 10, 26, 45–6, 76
Guchkov, Alexander 20–1, 28, 37

haemophilia 18–19, 20–1

Helphand-Parvus, Alexander 44–5,
47–8
Hoover, Herbert 74, 94–5

Imperial Russian Army; under tsar 5,
14, 24–5, 35–6
break up of 39–40, 41, 47, 51,
53–6, 79–80
industry 7–8, 29, 65, 70, 94
intelligentsia **10–11**
see also writers

Japan 13–14
Jewish people 6, 13, 16–17, 25, 38,
42–3

Kadets (Constitutional Democrats)
15, 28, 30, 66
Kamenev, Lev 41, 42, 58–9, 60
Kerensky, Alexander 33, 38, 50,
54–6, 59
Khrushchev, Nikita 105
Korean peninsula 13
Kornilov, General Lavr **53–6**
Kronstadt revolt **86–9**, 91, 96
Krupskaya, Nadezhda (Lenin's wife)
99

Labour army 83
Labour group (War Industries
Committee) 36, 38
Labour-Socialist Revolutionary
group 33
Latvian people 43

Lazovert, Dr Stanislaus 32
Left Communist group 84
Left Socialist Revolutionary Party 65,
    66
Lenin (Vladimir Ulyanov); ideology
    3–4, 9, 42–4, 95–7, 99–100
    Trench Pravda 54–5
    State and Revolution 69
    What is to be Done? 96
    before Revolution 40, 45, 47–50,
    51–2
    and Revolution **56–60**
    after Revolution 61, **63–70**, 71–97
    passim
Lithuania 25, 75
Lunacharsky, Anatoly 100–3
Lvov, Prince 45

Manchuria 13–14
Marxist theory 9, 10–11, 43–4, 69,
    85–6
Mensheviks **2–4**, 43–9 *passim*, 59–60,
    66, 68, 84
Michael, Grand Duke 32, 37–8
middle classes 7, 49, 62
migration 7, 68, 104
Milyukov, Paul 30–1
Minsk 75
Moscow 52–3, 71

NEP (New Economic Policy) **89–92**,
    93–4
Nicholas II, Tsar; character 22
    as ruler 13, 15, 16, 18, 24, 25–6
    abdication 32, 36–8, 51–2
    assassination 33, 71
Nikolai Nikolayevich, Grand Duke
    25–6
Octobrist Party 20

peasants; before Revolution **5–7**, 15
    after Revolution 65, 69–70, 74,
    79–82, **91–2**, 94
Peter the Great, Tsar 7
Petrograd *see* St Petersburg
Poland/Polish people 11, 25, 43, 63,
    64–5, **74–6**, 90
Politburo 61–2, 71, 86, 96–7
press 10–11, 21–2, 105–6
Progressive Bloc (Duma) 28, 30, 33
Provisional Government **45–50**, 52,
    55, **57–60**, 66
Purishkevich, Vladimir 31–2
Putilov armaments factory 35

railways 14, 52, 65
Rasputin, Gregory **18–22**, 26–7, **31–2**
Red Army 68, 73–4, 75, 82–3, 89, 94
Red Guards 57, 59
Red Terror 71–2
Rodzianko, Fedor 37
Romanov dynasty 19, 38
    see also Nicholas II
Russian Revolution (1905) 4
Russian Revolution (1917); summary
    vii–viii

October coup **56–60**
see also (principally) Bolsheviks;
   Lenin
Russian Social Democratic Workers'
   Party 2–3, 42

St Petersburg 7, 19, 24
   Petrograd (1914–24) 30, 32, 35–6,
   52–3, 63, 83, 100
   Petrograd Soviet **39–40**, **45–50**,
   54–6
Shulgin, Vasili 37
Socialist Realism 103
Soviet Union vii, 61, 67, 76, 105
Soviets (workers' councils) **38–40**,
   41, **45–50**, 54–60 *passim*, **61**, 79
Stalin, Joseph (Dzhugashvili) **41–2**,
   86, 89, 97, 105
Stolypin, Peter 17
Stuermer, Prime Minister 29–30
Sukhotin, Lieutenant Ivan 31–2

taxes 5, 47, 92
trade unions *see* workers
Treaty of Brest-Litovsk **64–6**, 71, 84,
   90
Treaty of Portsmouth 15
Treaty of Riga 76
Trotsky, Leon (Lev Bronstein); early
   years 38–9
   and Revolution **56–60**

after Revolution 61, **73-6**, 81, 85–6,
   88, 97
Tukhachevsky, General Mikhail 89

Ukraine/Ukrainians 43, 63, 64–5,
   66, 72, 76
United States of America 10, 14–15
   American Relief Administration
   74, 94–5
USSR *see* Soviet Union

Vilna 75

War Communism **69–70**, 85, 91–2
Warsaw 75
White Russian movement 67-8, **70–6**,
   77, 90
Winter Palace 59, 100
Witte, Sergei 14–15
workers **7–9**, 10–11, 49, 68, 78,
   83–6
world revolution 62–3
writers **103–4**, **105–6**

Yanushkevich, General 26
Young Turk movement 47
Yusupov, Prince Felix 31–2

zemstvos (land assemblies) 11–12
Zimmerwald Conference 40, 51–2
Zinoviev, Gregory 58–9